Learning the Par

Python Tools for Data Munging,
Analysis, and Visualization

Learning the Pandas Library

Python Tools for Data Munging, Analysis, and Visualization

Matt Harrison

Technical Editor: Michael Prentiss

hairysun.com

COPYRIGHT © 2016

While every precaution has been taken in the preparation of this book, the publisher and author assumes no responsibility for errors or omissions, or for damages resulting from the use of the information contained herein

Contents

1 Introduction — 3
 1.1 Who this book is for — 4
 1.2 Data in this Book — 4
 1.3 Hints, Tables, and Images — 4

2 Installation — 5
 2.1 Other Installation Options — 6
 2.2 `scipy.stats` — 7
 2.3 Summary — 7

3 Data Structures — 9
 3.1 Summary — 10

4 Series — 11
 4.1 The index abstraction — 12
 4.2 The pandas `Series` — 12
 4.3 The NaN value — 15
 4.4 Similar to NumPy — 16
 4.5 Summary — 17

5 Series CRUD — 19
 5.1 Creation — 19
 5.2 Reading — 20
 5.3 Updating — 22
 5.4 Deletion — 23
 5.5 Summary — 24

6 Series Indexing — 25
 6.1 `.iloc` and `.loc` — 27
 6.2 `.at` and `.iat` — 29
 6.3 `.ix` — 30
 6.4 Indexing Summary — 30
 6.5 Slicing — 31
 6.6 Boolean Arrays — 31

v

CONTENTS

    6.7 Summary 33

7 Series Methods   **35**
    7.1 Iteration 35
    7.2 Overloaded operations 37
    7.3 Getting and Setting Values 39
    7.4 Reset Index 43
    7.5 Counts 45
    7.6 Statistics 47
    7.7 Convert Types 52
    7.8 Dealing with None 53
    7.9 Matrix Operations 55
    7.10 Append, combining, and joining two series 56
    7.11 Sorting 57
    7.12 Applying a function 59
    7.13 Serialization 61
    7.14 String operations 63
    7.15 Summary 64

8 Series Plotting   **67**
    8.1 Other plot types 71
    8.2 Summary 73

9 Another Series Example   **75**
    9.1 Standard Python 75
    9.2 Enter pandas 78
    9.3 Tweaking data 79
    9.4 Custom symbol frequency 81
    9.5 Summary 83

10 DataFrames   **85**
    10.1 DataFrames 86
    10.2 Construction 88
    10.3 Data Frame Axis 89
    10.4 Summary 90

11 Data Frame Example   **91**
    11.1 Looking at the data 94
    11.2 Plotting With Data Frames 95
    11.3 Adding rows 98
    11.4 Adding columns 100
    11.5 Deleting Rows 101
    11.6 Deleting Columns 102
    11.7 Summary 103

12 Data Frame Methods   **105**
    12.1 Data Frame Attributes 105

Contents

    12.2 Iteration 106
    12.3 Arithmetic 109
    12.4 Matrix Operations 110
    12.5 Serialization 111
    12.6 Index Operations 113
    12.7 Getting and Setting Values 114
    12.8 Deleting Columns 116
    12.9 Slicing 118
    12.10 Sorting 121
    12.11 Summary 122

13 Data Frame Statistics   **123**
    13.1 describe and quantile 124
    13.2 rank 126
    13.3 clip 127
    13.4 Correlation and Covariance 128
    13.5 Reductions 128
    13.6 Summary 130

14 Grouping, Pivoting, and Reshaping   **131**
    14.1 Reducing Methods in groupby 131
    14.2 Pivot Tables 134
    14.3 Melting Data 136
    14.4 Converting Back to Wide 139
    14.5 Creating Dummy Variables 140
    14.6 Undoing Dummy Variables 141
    14.7 Stacking and Unstacking 141
    14.8 Summary 141

15 Dealing With Missing Data   **145**
    15.1 Finding Missing Data 146
    15.2 Dropping Missing Data 147
    15.3 Inserting Data for Missing Data 148
    15.4 Summary 151

16 Joining Data Frames   **153**
    16.1 Adding Rows to Data Frames 153
    16.2 Adding Columns to Data Frames 154
    16.3 Joins 155
    16.4 Summary 157

17 Avalanche Analysis and Plotting   **159**
    17.1 Getting Data 159
    17.2 Munging Data 164
    17.3 Describing Data 166
    17.4 Categorical Data 168
    17.5 Converting Column Types 169

17.6 Dealing with Dates 171
17.7 Splitting a Column into Two Columns 173
17.8 Analysis 175
17.9 Plotting on Maps 177
17.10 Bar Plots 179
17.11 Assorted Plots 182
17.12 Summary 185

18 Summary   **187**

About the Author   **189**

Index   **191**

Also Available   **198**
   Beginning Python Programming 198
   Reviews 199
   Treading on Python: Vol 2: Intermediate Python 201
   Reviews 202

Forward

Python is easy to learn. You can learn the basics in a day and be productive with it. With only an understanding of Python, moving to pandas can be difficult or confusing. This book is meant to aid you in mastering pandas.

I have taught Python and pandas to many people over the years, in large corporate environments, small startups, and in Python and Data Science conferences. I have seen what hangs people up, and confuses them. With the correct background, an attitude of acceptance, and a deep breath, much of this confusion evaporates.

Having said this, pandas is an excellent tool. Many are using it around the world to great success. I hope you do as well.

Cheers!
Matt

Chapter 1

Introduction

I have been using Python is some professional capacity since the turn of the century. One of the trends that I have seen in that time is the uptake of Python for various aspects of "data science"- gathering data, cleaning data, analysis, machine learning, and visualization. The pandas library has seen much uptake in this area.

pandas[1] is a data analysis library for Python that has exploded in popularity over the past years. The website describes it thusly:

> "pandas is an open source, BSD-licensed library providing high-performance, easy-to-use data structures and data analysis tools for the Python programming language."
>
> -pandas.pydata.org

My description of pandas is: pandas is an in memory nosql database, that has sql-like constructs, basic statistical and analytic support, as well as graphing capability. Because it is built on top of Cython, it has less memory overhead and runs quicker. Many people are using pandas to replace Excel, perform ETL, process tabular data, load CSV or JSON files, and more. Though it grew out of the financial sector (for analysis of time series data), it is now a general purpose data manipulation library.

Because pandas has some lineage back to NumPy, it adopts some NumPy'isms that normal Python programmers may not be aware of or familiar with. Certainly, one could go out and use Cython to perform fast typed data analysis with a Python-like dialect, but with pandas, you don't need to. This work is done for you. If you are

---

[1] pandas (http://pandas.pydata.org) refers to itself in lowercase, so this book will follow suit.

using pandas and the vectorized operations, you are getting close to C level speeds, but writing Python.

1.1 Who this book is for

This guide is intended to introduce pandas to Python programmers. It covers many (but not all) aspects, as well as some gotchas or details that may be counter-intuitive or even non-pythonic to longtime users of Python.

This book assumes basic knowledge of Python. The author has written *Treading on Python Vol 1*[2] that provides all the background necessary.

1.2 Data in this Book

Some might complain that the datasets in this book are small. That is true, and in some cases (as in plotting a histogram), that is a drawback. On the other hand, every attempt has been made to have real data that illustrates using pandas and the features found in it. As a visual learner, I appreciate seeing where data is coming and going. As such, I try to shy away from just showing tables of random numbers that have no meaning.

1.3 Hints, Tables, and Images

The hints, tables, and graphics found in this book, have been collected over almost five years of using pandas. They are derived from hangups, notes, and cheatsheets that I have developed after using pandas and teaching others how to use it. Hopefully, they are useful to you as well.

In the physical version of this book, is an index that has also been battle-tested during development. Inevitably, when I was doing analysis not related to the book, I would check that the index had the information I needed. If it didn't, I added it. Let me know if you find any omissions!

Finally, having been around the publishing block and releasing content to the world, I realize that I probably have many omissions that others might consider required knowledge. Many will enjoy the content, others might have the opposite reaction. If you have feedback, or suggestions for improvement, please reach out to me. I love to hear back from readers! Your comments will improve future versions.

---

[2] http://hairysun.com/books/tread/

Chapter 2

Installation

Python 3 has been out for a while now, and people claim it is the future. As an attempt to be modern, this book will use Python 3 throughout! Do not despair, the code will run in Python 2 as well. In fact, review versions of the book neglected to list the Python version, and there was a single complaint about a superfluous list(range(10)) call. The lone line of (Python 2) code required for compatibility is:

```
>>> from __future__ import print_function
```

Having gotten that out of the way, let's address installation of pandas. The easiest and least painful way to install pandas on most platforms is to use the Anaconda distribution[3]. Anaconda is a meta distribution of Python, that contains many additional packages that have traditionally been annoying to install unless you have toolchains to compile Fortran and C code. Anaconda allows you to skip the compile step and provides binaries for most platforms. The Anaconda distribution itself is freely available, though commercial support is available as well.

After installing the Anaconda package, you should have a conda executable. Running:

```
$ conda install pandas
```

Will install pandas and any dependencies. To verify that this works, simply try to import the pandas package:

```
$ python
>>> import pandas
>>> pandas.__version__
'0.18.0'
```

2. INSTALLATION

If the library successfully imports, you should be good to go.

2.1 Other Installation Options

The pandas library will install on Windows, Mac, and Linux via pip[4].

Mac and Windows users wishing to install binaries may download them from the pandas website. Most Linux distributions also have native packages pre-built and available in their repos. On Ubuntu and Debian apt-get will install the library:

```
$ sudo apt-get install python-pandas
```

Pandas can also be installed from source. I feel the need to advise you that you might spend a bit of time going down this rabbit hole if you are not familiar with getting compiler toolchains installed on your system.

It may be necessary to prep the environment for building pandas from source by installing dependencies and the proper header files for Python. On Ubuntu this is straightforward, other environments may be different:

```
$ sudo apt-get install build-essential python-all-dev
```

Using virtualenv[5] will alleviate the need for superuser access during installation. Because virtualenv uses pip, it can download and install newer releases of pandas if the version found on the distribution is lagging.

On Mac and Linux platforms, the following create a virtualenv sandbox and installs the latest pandas in it (assuming that the prerequisite files are also installed):

```
$ virtualenv pandas-env
$ source pandas-env/bin/activate
$ pip install pandas
```

After a while, pandas should be ready for use. Try to import the library and check the version:

```
$ source pandas-env/bin/activate
$ python
>>> import pandas
>>> pandas.__version__
'0.18.0'
```

---

[3] https://www.continuum.io/downloads

[4] http://pip-installer.org/

2.2 scipy.stats

Some nicer plotting features require scipy.stats. This library is not required, but pandas will complain if the user tries to perform an action that has this dependency. scipy.stats has many non-Python dependencies and in practice turns out to be a little more involved to install. For Ubuntu, the following packages are required before a pip install scipy will work:

```
$ sudo apt-get install libatlas-base-dev gfortran
```

Installation of these dependencies is sufficiently annoying that it has lead to "complete scientific Python offerings", such as Anaconda [6]. These installers bundle many libraries, are available for Linux, Mac, and Windows, and have optional support contracts. They are a great way to quickly get an environment up.

2.3 Summary

Unlike "pure" Python modules, pandas is not just a pip install away unless you have an environment configured to build it. The easiest was to get going is to use the Anaconda Python distribution. Having said that, it is certainly possible to install pandas using other methods.

---

[5]http://www.virtualenv.org

[6]https://store.continuum.io/cshop/anaconda/

Chapter 3

Data Structures

One of the keys to understanding pandas is to understand the data model. At the core of pandas are three data structures:

Data Structure	Dimensionality	Spreadsheet Analog
Series	1D	Column
DataFrame	2D	Single Sheet
Panel	3D	Multiple Sheets

Figure 3.1: Different dimensions of pandas data structures

The most widely used data structures are the Series and the DataFrame that deal with array data and tabular data respectively. An analogy with the spreadsheet world illustrates the basic differences between these types. A DataFrame is similar to a sheet with rows and columns, while a Series is similar to a single column of data. A Panel is a group of sheets. Likewise, in pandas a Panel can have many DataFrames, each which in turn may have multiple Series.

Diving into these core data structures a little more is useful because a bit of understanding goes a long way towards better use of the library. This book will ignore the Panel, because I have yet to see anyone use it in the real world. On the other hand, we will spend a good portion of time discussing the Series and DataFrame. Both the Series and DataFrame share features. For example they both have an index, which we will need to examine to really understand how pandas works.

Also, because the DataFrame can be thought of as a collection of columns that are really Series objects, it is imperative that we have a comprehensive study of the Series first. Additionally, we see this when we iterate over rows, and the rows are represented as Series.

9

3. Data Structures

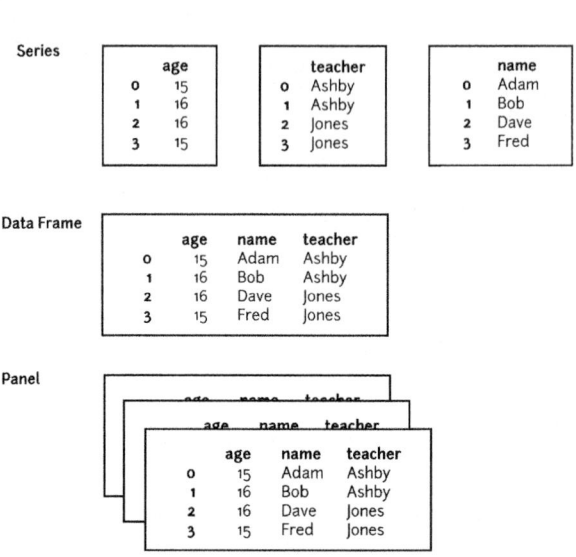

Figure 3.2: Figure showing relation between main data structures in pandas. Namely, that a data frame can have multiple series, and a panel has multiple data frames.

Some have compared the data structures to Python lists or dictionaries, and I think this is a stretch that doesn't provide much benefit. Mapping the list and dictionary methods on top of pandas' data structures just leads to confusion.

3.1 Summary

The pandas library includes three main data structures and associated functions for manipulating them. This book will focus on the `Series` and `DataFrame`. First, we will look at the `Series` as the `DataFrame` can be thought of as a collection of `Series`.

Chapter 4

Series

A `Series` is used to model one dimensional data, similar to a list in Python. The `Series` object also has a few more bits of data, including an index and a name. A common idea through pandas is the notion of an axis. Because a series is one dimensional, it has a single *axis*—the index.

Below is a table of counts of songs artists composed:

Artist	Data
0	145
1	142
2	38
3	13

To represent this data in pure Python, you could use a data structure similar to the one that follows. It is a dictionary that has a list of the data points, stored under the `'data'` key. In addition to an entry in the dictionary for the actual data, there is an explicit entry for the corresponding index values for the data (in the `'index'` key), as well as an entry for the name of the data (in the `'name'` key):

```
>>> ser = {
...     'index':[0, 1, 2, 3],
...     'data':[145, 142, 38, 13],
...     'name':'songs'
... }
```

The get function defined below can pull items out of this data structure based on the index:

```
>>> def get(ser, idx):
...     value_idx = ser['index'].index(idx)
...     return ser['data'][value_idx]
```

11

4. Series

```
>>> get(ser, 1)
142
```

Note

The code samples in this book are generally shown as if they were typed directly into an interpreter. Lines starting with >>> and ... are interpreter markers for the *input prompt* and *continuation prompt* respectively. Lines that are not prefixed by one of those sequences are the output from the interpreter after running the code.

The Python interpreter will print the return value of the last invocation (even if the print statement is missing) automatically. To use the code samples found in this book, leave the interpreter markers out.

4.1 The index abstraction

This double abstraction of the index seems unnecessary at first glance—a list already has integer indexes. But there is a trick up pandas' sleeves. By allowing non-integer values, the data structure actually supports other index types such as strings, dates, as well as arbitrary ordered indices or even duplicate index values.

Below is an example that has string values for the index:

```
>>> songs = {
...     'index':['Paul', 'John', 'George', 'Ringo'],
...     'data':[145, 142, 38, 13],
...     'name':'counts'
...     }
>>> get(songs, 'John')
142
```

The index is a core feature of pandas' data structures given the library's past in analysis of financial data or *time series data*. Many of the operations performed on a Series operate directly on the index or by index lookup.

4.2 The pandas Series

With that background in mind, let's look at how to create a Series in pandas. It is easy to create a Series object from a list:

```
>>> import pandas as pd
>>> songs2 = pd.Series([145, 142, 38, 13],
...         name='counts')
```

4.2. The pandas Series

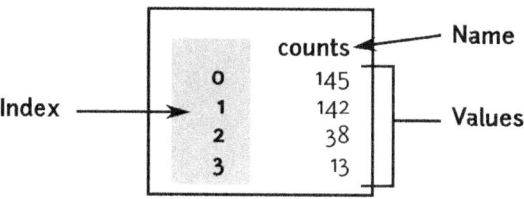

Figure 4.1: Figure showing the parts of a Series.

```
>>> songs2
0    145
1    142
2     38
3     13
Name: counts, dtype: int64
```

When the interpreter prints our series, pandas makes a best effort to format it for the current terminal size. The left most column is the *index* column which contains entries for the index. The generic name for an index is an *axis*, and the values of the index—0, 1, 2, 3—are called *axis labels*. The two dimensional structure in pandas—a DataFrame—has two axes, one for the rows and another for the columns.

The rightmost column in the output contains the *values* of the series. In this case, they are integers (the console representation says dtype: int64, dtype meaning data type, and int64 meaning 64 bit integer), but in general values of a Series can hold strings, floats, booleans, or arbitrary Python objects. To get the best speed (such as vectorized operations), the values should be of the same type, though this is not required.

It is easy to inspect the index of a series (or data frame), as it is an attribute of the object:

4. Series

```
>>> songs2.index
RangeIndex(start=0, stop=4, step=1)
```

The default values for an index are monotonically increasing integers. songs2 has an integer based index.

Note

The index can be string based as well, in which case pandas indicates that the datatype for the index is object (not string):

```
>>> songs3 = pd.Series([145, 142, 38, 13],
...     name='counts',
...     index=['Paul', 'John', 'George', 'Ringo'])
```

Note that the dtype that we see when we print a Series is the type of the values, not of the index:

```
>>> songs3
Paul      145
John      142
George     38
Ringo      13
Name: counts, dtype: int64
```

When we inspect the index attribute, we see that the dtype is object:

```
>>> songs3.index
Index(['Paul', 'John', 'George', 'Ringo'],
dtype='object')
```

The actual data for a series does not have to be numeric or homogeneous. We can insert Python objects into a series:

```
>>> class Foo:
...     pass
>>> ringo = pd.Series(
...     ['Richard', 'Starkey', 13, Foo()],
...     name='ringo')
>>> ringo
0                         Richard
1                         Starkey
2                              13
3     <__main__.Foo instance at 0x...>
Name: ringo, dtype: object
```

In the above case, the dtype-*datatype*-of the Series is object (meaning a Python object). This can be good or bad.

The object data type is used for strings. But, it is also used for values that have heterogenous types. If you have numeric data, you wouldn't want it to be stored as a Python object, but rather as an `int64` or `float64`, which allow you to do vectorized numeric operations.

If you have time data and it says it has the `object` type, you probably have strings for the dates. This is bad as you don't get the date operations that you would get if the type were `datetime64[ns]`. Strings on the other hand, are stored in pandas as `object`. Don't worry, we will see how to convert types later in the book.

4.3 The NaN value

A value that may be familiar to NumPy users, but not Python users in general, is NaN. When pandas determines that a series holds numeric values, but it cannot find a number to represent an entry, it will use NaN. This value stands for *Not A Number*, and is usually ignored in arithmetic operations. (Similar to NULL in SQL).

Here is a series that has NaN in it:

```
>>> nan_ser = pd.Series([2, None],
...      index=['Ono', 'Clapton'])
>>> nan_ser
Ono        2.0
Clapton    NaN
dtype: float64
```

> **Note**
>
> One thing to note is that the type of this series is `float64`, not `int64`! This is because the only numeric column that supports NaN is the float column. When pandas sees numeric data (2) as well as the None, it coerced the 2 to a float value.

Below is an example of how pandas ignores NaN. The `.count` method, which counts the number of values in a series, disregards NaN. In this case, it indicates that the count of items in the `Series` is one, one for the value of 2 at index location `Ono`, ignoring the NaN value at index location `Clapton`:

```
>>> nan_ser.count()
1
```

> **Note**
>
> If you load data from a CSV file, an empty value for an otherwise numeric column will become NaN. Later, methods such as `.fillna` and `.dropna` will explain how to deal with NaN.

None, NaN, nan, and null are synonyms in this book when referring to empty or missing data found in a pandas series or data frame.

4. Series

4.4 Similar to NumPy

The `Series` object behaves similarly to a NumPy array. As show below, both types respond to index operations:

```
>>> import numpy as np
>>> numpy_ser = np.array([145, 142, 38, 13])
>>> songs3[1]
142
>>> numpy_ser[1]
142
```

They both have methods in common:

```
>>> songs3.mean()
84.5
>>> numpy_ser.mean()
84.5
```

They also both have a notion of a *boolean array*. This is a boolean expression that is used as a mask to filter out items. Normal Python lists do not support such fancy index operations:

```
>>> mask = songs3 > songs3.median()  # boolean array
>>> mask
Paul       True
John       True
George     False
Ringo      False
Name: counts, dtype: bool
```

Once we have a mask, we can use that to filter out items of the sequence, by performing an index operation. If the mask has a `True` value for a given index, the value is kept. Otherwise, the value is dropped. The mask above represents the locations that have a value greater than the median value of the series.

```
>>> songs3[mask]
Paul    145
John    142
Name: counts, dtype: int64
```

NumPy also has filtering by boolean arrays, but lacks the `.median` method on an array. Instead, NumPy provides a `median` function in the NumPy namespace:

```
>>> numpy_ser[numpy_ser > np.median(numpy_ser)]
array([145, 142])
```

Note

Both NumPy and pandas have adopted the convention of using import statements in combination with an as statement to rename their imports to two letter acronyms:

```
>>> import pandas as pd
>>> import numpy as np
```

This removes some typing while still allowing the user to be explicit with their namespaces.

Be careful, as you may see to following cast about in code samples:

```
>>> from pandas import *
```

Though you see *star imports* frequently used in examples online, I would advise not to use star imports. They have the potential to clobber items in your namespace and make tracing the source of a definition more difficult (especially if you have multiple star imports). As the Zen of Python states, "Explicit is better than implicit"[7].

4.5 Summary

The Series object is a one dimensional data structure. It can hold numerical data, time data, strings, or arbitrary Python objects. If you are dealing with numeric data, using pandas rather than a Python list will give you additional benefits as it is faster, consumes less memory, and comes with built-in methods that are very useful to manipulate the data. In addition, the index abstraction allows for accessing values by position or label. A Series can also have empty values, and has some similarities to NumPy arrays. This is the basic workhorse of pandas, mastering it will pay dividends.

---

[7]Type import this into an interpreter to see the Zen of Python. Or search for "PEP 20".

Chapter 5

Series CRUD

The pandas Series data structure provides support for the basic CRUD operations—create, read, update, and delete. One thing to be aware of is that in general pandas objects tend to behave in an immutable manner. Although they are mutable, you don't normally update a series, but rather perform an operation that will return a new Series. Exceptions to this are noted throughout the book.

5.1 Creation

It is easy to create a series from a Python list of values. Here we create a series with the count of songs attributed to George Harrison during the final years of The Beatles and the release of his 1970 album, *All Things Must Pass*. The index is specified as the second parameter using a list of string years as values. Note that 1970 is included once for George's work as a member of the Beatles and repeated for his solo album:

```
>>> george_dupe = pd.Series([10, 7, 1, 22],
...     index=['1968', '1969', '1970', '1970'],
...     name='George Songs')
>>> george_dupe
1968    10
1969     7
1970     1
1970    22
Name: George Songs, dtype: int64
```

The previous example illustrates an interesting feature of pandas—the index values are strings and they are not unique. This can cause some confusion, but can also be useful when duplicate index items are needed.

5. Series CRUD

This series was created with a list and an explicit index. A series can also be created with a dictionary that maps index entries to values. If a dictionary is used, an additional sequence containing the order of the index is mandatory. This last parameter is necessary because a Python dictionary is not ordered.

For our current data, creating this series from a dictionary is less powerful, because it cannot place different values in a series for the same index label (a dictionary has unique keys and we are using the keys as index labels). One might attempt to get around this by mapping the label to a list of values, but these attempts will fail. The list of values will be interpreted as a Python list, not two separate entries:

```
>>> g2 = pd.Series({'1969': 7, '1970': [1, 22]},
...                 index=['1969', '1970', '1970'])
>>> g2
1969           7
1970      [1, 22]
1970      [1, 22]
dtype: object
```

Tip

If you need to have multiple values for an index entry, use a list to specify both the index and values.

5.2 Reading

To read or select the data from a series, one can simply use an index operation in combination with the index entry:

```
>>> george_dupe['1968']
10
```

Normally this returns a scalar value. However, in the case where index entries repeat, this is not the case! Here, the result will be another `Series` object:

```
# may not be a scalar!
>>> george_dupe['1970']
1970     1
1970    22
Name: George Songs, dtype: int64
```

5.2. Reading

Note

Care must be taken when working with data that has non-unique index values. Scalar values and `Series` objects have a different interface, and trying to treat them the same will lead to errors.

We can iterate over data in a series as well. When iterating over a series, we loop over the values of the series:

```
>>> for item in george_dupe:
...     print(item)
10
7
1
22
```

However, though *iteration* (looping over the values via the `.__iter__` method) occurs over the values of a series, *membership* (checking for value in the series with the `.__contains__` method) is against the index items. Neither Python lists nor dictionaries behave this way. If you wanted to know if the value 22 was in george_dupe, you might fall victim to an erroneous result if you think you can simply use the `in` test for membership:

```
>>> 22 in george_dupe
False
```

To test a series for membership, test against the `set` of the series or the `.values` attribute:

```
>>> 22 in set(george_dupe)
True

>>> 22 in george_dupe.values
True
```

This can be tricky, remember that in a series, *although iteration is over the values of the series, membership is over the index names*:

```
>>> '1970' in george_dupe
True
```

To iterate over the tuples containing both the index label and the value, use the `.iteritems` method:

```
>>> for item in george_dupe.iteritems():
...     print(item)
('1968', 10)
('1969', 7)
('1970', 1)
('1970', 22)
```

21

5. Series CRUD

5.3 Updating

Updating values in a series can be a little tricky as well. To update a value for a given index label, the standard index assignment operation works and performs the update in-place (in effect mutating the series):

```
>>> george_dupe['1969'] = 6
>>> george_dupe['1969']
6
```

The index assignment operation also works to add a new index and a value. Here we add the count of songs for his 1973 album, *Living in a Material World*:

```
>>> george_dupe['1973'] = 11
>>> george_dupe
1968    10
1969     6
1970     1
1970    22
1973    11
Name: George Songs, dtype: int64
```

Because an index operation either updates or appends, one must be aware of the data they are dealing with. Be careful if you intend to add a value with an index entry that already exists in the series. Assignment via an index operation to an existing index entry will overwrite previous entries.

Notice what happens when we try to update an index that has duplicate entries. Say we found an extra Beatles song in 1970 attributed to George, and wanted to update the entry that held 1 to 2:

```
>>> george_dupe['1970'] = 2

>>> george_dupe
1968    10
1969     6
1970     2
1970     2
1973    11
Name: George Songs, dtype: int64
```

Both values for 1970 were set to 2. If you had to deal with data such as this, it would probably be better to use a data frame with a column for artist (i.e. Beatles, or George Harrison) or a multi-index (described later). To update values based purely on position, perform an index assignment of the .iloc attribute:

```
>>> george_dupe.iloc[3] = 22
>>> george_dupe
```

22

```
1968     10
1969      6
1970      2
1970     22
1973     11
Name: George Songs, dtype: int64
```

Note

There is an .append method on the series object, but it does not behave like the Python list's .append method. It is somewhat analogous the Python list's .extend method in that it expects another series to append to:

```
>>> george_dupe.append(pd.Series({'1974':9}))
1968     10
1969      6
1970      2
1970     22
1973     11
1974      9
dtype: int64
```

In this case, we keep the original series intact and a new Series object is returned as the result. Note that the name of the george series is not carried over into the new series.

The series object has a .set_value method that will *both* add a new item to the existing series and return a series:

```
>>> george_dupe.set_value('1974', 9)
1968     10
1969      6
1970      2
1970     22
1973     11
1974      9
Name: George Songs, dtype: int64
```

5.4 Deletion

Deletion is not common in the pandas world. It is more common to use filters or masks to create a new series that has only the items that you want. However, if you really want to remove entries, you can delete based on index entries.

Recent versions of pandas support the del statement, which deletes based on the index:

```
>>> del george_dupe['1973']

>>> george_dupe
```

5. Series CRUD

```
1968    10
1969     6
1970     2
1970    22
1974     9
Name: George Songs, dtype: int64
```

Note

The del statement appears to have problems with duplicate index values (as of version 0.14.1):

```
>>> s = pd.Series([2, 3, 4], index=[1, 2, 1])
>>> del s[1]

>>> s
1    4
dtype: int64
```

One might assume that del would remove any entries with that index value. For some reason, it also appears to have removed index 2 but left the second index 1.

To delete values from a series, it is more common to *filter* the series to get a new series. Here is a basic filter that returns all values less than or equal to 2. The example below uses a *boolean array* inlined into the index operation. This is common in NumPy but not supported in normal Python lists or dictionaries:

```
>>> george_dupe[george_dupe <= 2]
1970    2
Name: George Songs, dtype: int64
```

5.5 Summary

A Series doesn't just hold data. It allows you to get at the data, update it, or remove it. Often, we perform this operations through the index. We have just scratched the surface in this chapter. In future chapters, we will dive deeper into the Series.

Chapter 6

Series Indexing

This section will discuss indexing best practices. As illustrated with our example series, the index does not have to be whole numbers. Here we use strings for the index:

```
>>> george = pd.Series([10, 7],
...     index=['1968', '1969'],
...     name='George Songs')
>>> george
1968    10
1969     7
Name: George Songs, dtype: int64
```

george's index type is object (pandas indicates that strings index entries are objects), note the dtype of the index attribute:

```
>>> george.index
Index(['1968', '1969'], dtype='object')
```

We have previously seen that indexes do not have to be unique. To determine whether an index has duplicates, simply inspect the .is_unique attribute on the index:

```
>>> dupe = pd.Series([10, 2, 7],
...     index=['1968', '1968', '1969'],
...     name='George Songs')
>>> dupe.index.is_unique
False

>>> george.index.is_unique
True
```

25

6. Series Indexing

Much like numpy arrays, a `Series` object can be both indexed and sliced along the axis. *Indexing* pulls out either a scalar or multiple values (if there are non-unique index labels):

```
>>> george
1968    10
1969     7
Name: George Songs, dtype: int64

>>> george[0]
10
```

The indexing rules are somewhat complex. They behave more like a dictionary, but in the case where a string index label (rather than integer based indexing) is used, the behavior falls back to Python list indexing. Yes, this is confusing. Some examples might help to clarify. The series george has non-numeric indexes:

```
>>> george['1968']
10
```

This series can also be indexed by position (using integers) even though it has string index entries! The first item is at key 0, and the last item is at key -1:

```
>>> george[0]
10

>>> george[-1]
7
```

What is going on? Indexing with strings and integers!? Because this is confusing and in Python, "explicit is better than implicit", the pandas documentation actually suggests indexing based off of the .loc and .iloc attributes rather than indexing the object directly:

> While standard Python / Numpy expressions for selecting and setting are intuitive and come in handy for interactive work, for production code, we recommend the optimized pandas data access methods, .at, .iat, .loc, .iloc and .ix.
>
> pandas website[8]

---

[8]http://pandas.pydata.org/pandas-docs/stable/10min.html

Note

As we have see, the result of an index operation may not be a scalar. If the index labels are not unique, it is possible that the index operation returns a sub-series rather than a scalar value:

```
>>> dupe
1968    10
1968     2
1969     7
Name: George Songs, dtype: int64

>>> dupe['1968']
1968    10
1968     2
Name: George Songs, dtype: int64

>>> dupe['1969']
7
```

This is a potential issue if you are assuming the result of your data to be only scalar and have duplicate labels in the index.

Note

If the index is already using integer labels, then the fallback to position based indexing does not work!:

```
>>> george_i = pd.Series([10, 7],
...     index=[1968, 1969],
...     name='George Songs')

>>> george_i[-1]
Traceback (most recent call last):
   ...
KeyError: -1
```

6.1 .iloc and .loc

The optimized data access methods are accessed by indexing off of the .loc and .iloc attributes. These two attributes allow label-based and position-based indexing respectively.

When we perform an index operation on the .iloc attribute, it does lookup based on *index* position (in this case pandas behaves similar to a Python list). pandas will raise an IndexError if there is no index at that location:

```
>>> george.iloc[0]
10
```

6. SERIES INDEXING

```
>>> george.iloc[-1]
7

>>> george.iloc[4]
Traceback (most recent call last):
    ...
IndexError: single positional indexer is out-of-bounds

>>> george.iloc['1968']
Traceback (most recent call last):
    ...
TypeError: cannot do positional indexing on <class
'pandas.indexes.base.Index'> with these indexers [1968]
of <class 'str'>
```

In addition to pulling out a single item, we can slice just like in normal Python:

```
>>> george.iloc[0:3]    # slice
1968    10
1969     7
Name: George Songs, dtype: int64
```

Additional functionality not found in normal Python is indexing based off of a list. You can pass in a list of index locations to the index operation:

```
>>> george.iloc[[0,1]]   # list
1968    10
1969     7
Name: George Songs, dtype: int64
```

.loc is supposed to be based on the index labels and not the positions. As such, it is analogous to Python dictionary-based indexing. Though it has some additional functionality, as it can accept boolean arrays, slices, and a list of labels (none of which work with a Python dictionary):

```
>>> george.loc['1968']
10

>>> george.loc['1970']
Traceback (most recent call last):
    ...
KeyError: 'the label [1970] is not in the [index]'

>>> george.loc[0]
Traceback (most recent call last):
    ...
TypeError: cannot do label indexing on
<class 'pandas.indexes.base.Index'> with these
indexers [0] of <class 'int'>
```

Indexing

Figure 6.1: Figure showing how `iloc` and `loc` behave.

```
>>> george.loc[['1968', '1970']]   # list
1968    10.0
1970     NaN
Name: George Songs, dtype: float64

>>> george.loc['1968':]   # slice
1968    10
1969     7
Name: George Songs, dtype: int64
```

If you get confused by .loc and .iloc, remember that .iloc is based the index (starting with i) position. .loc is based on label (starting with l).

6.2 .at and .iat

The .at and .iat index accessors are analogous to .loc and .iloc. The difference being that they will return a numpy.ndarray when pulling out a duplicate value, whereas .loc and .iloc return a Series:

```
>>> george_dupe = pd.Series([10, 7, 1, 22],
...        index=['1968', '1969', '1970', '1970'],
...        name='George Songs')

>>> george_dupe.at['1970']
array([ 1, 22])

>>> george_dupe.loc['1970']
1970     1
1970    22
Name: George Songs, dtype: int64
```

6. Series Indexing

6.3 `.ix`

`.ix` is similar to `[]` indexing. Because it tries to support both positional and label based indexing, I advise against its' use in general. It tends to lead to confusing results and violates the notion that "explicit is better than implicit":

```
>>> george_dupe.ix[0]
10
>>> george_dupe.ix['1970']
1970     1
1970    22
Name: George Songs, dtype: int64
```

The case where `.ix` turns out to be useful is given in the pandas documentation:

> `.ix` is exceptionally useful when dealing with mixed positional and label based hierachical indexes.

If you are using pivot tables, or stacking (as described later), `.ix` can be useful. Note that the pandas documentation continues:

> However, when an axis is integer based, *only* label based access and not positional access is supported. Thus, in such cases, it's usually better to be explicit and use `.iloc` or `.loc`.

6.4 Indexing Summary

The following table summarizes the indexing methods and offers advice as to when to use them:

Method	When to Use
Attribute access	Getting values for a single index name when the name is a valid attribute name.
Index access	Getting/setting values for a single index name when the name is not a valid attribute names.
`.iloc`	Getting/setting values by index position or location. (Half-open interval for slices)
`.loc`	Getting/setting values by index label. (Closed interval for slices)
`.ix`	Getting/setting values by index label first, then falls back to position. Avoid unless you have hierarchical indexes that mix position and label indexes.
`.iat`	Getting/setting numpy array results by index position.
`.at`	Getting/setting numpy array results by index label.

6.5 Slicing

As mentioned, slicing can be performed on the index attributes—.iloc and .loc. Slicing attempts to pull out a range of index locations, and the result is a series, rather than a scalar item at a single index location (assuming unique index keys).

Slices take the form of [start]:[end][:stride] where start, end, and stride are integers and the square brackets represent optional values. The table below explains slicing possibilities for .iloc:

Slice	Result
0:1	First item
:1	First item (start default is 0)
:-2	Take from the start up to the second to last item
::2	Take from start to the end skipping every other item

The following example returns the values found at index position zero up to but not including index position two:

```
>>> george.iloc[0:2]
1968    10
1969     7
Name: George Songs, dtype: int64
```

6.6 Boolean Arrays

A slice using the result of a boolean operation is called a *boolean array*. It returns a filtered series for which the boolean operation is evaluated. Below a boolean array is assigned to a variable—mask:

```
>>> mask = george > 7
>>> mask
1968    True
1969    False
Name: George Songs, dtype: bool
```

Note

Boolean arrays might be confusing for programmers used to Python, but not NumPy. Taking a series and applying an operation to each value of the series is known as *broadcasting*. The > operation is broadcasted, or applied, to every entry in the series. And the result is a new series with the result of each of those operations. Because the result of applying the greater

31

6. Series Indexing

Masks

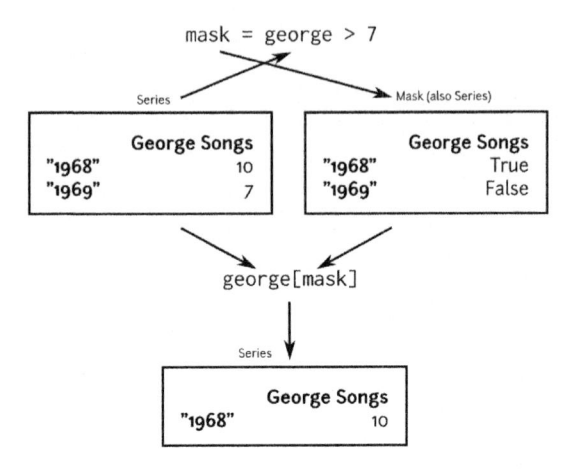

Figure 6.2: Figure showing creation and application of a mask to a Series. (Note that the mask itself is a Series as well).

than operator to each value returns a boolean, the final result is a new series with the same index labels as the original, but each value is True or False. This is referred to as a boolean array.

We can perform other broadcasting operations to a series. Here we increment the numerical values by adding two to them:

```
>>> george + 2
1968    12
1969     9
Name: George Songs, dtype: int64
```

When the mask is combined with an index operation, it returns a Series where only the items in the same position as True are returned:

```
>>> george[mask]
1968    10
Name: George Songs, dtype: int64
```

Multiple boolean operations can be combined with the following operations:

Operation	Example
And	ser[a & b]
Or	ser[a | b]
Not	ser[~a]

A potential gotcha with boolean arrays is operator precedence. If the masks are inlined into the index operation, it is best to surround them with parentheses. Below are non-inlined masks which function fine:

```
>>> mask2 = george <= 2
>>> george[mask | mask2]
1968    10
Name: George Songs, dtype: int64
```

Yet, when the mask operation is inlined, we encounter problems. Below is an example where operator precedence does not raise an error (it used to prior to 0.14), but is wrong! We asked for song count greater than seven or less than or equal to 2:

```
>>> george[mask | george <= 2]
1968    10
1969     7
Name: George Songs, dtype: int64
```

By wrapping the masks in parentheses, the correct order of operations is used, and the result is correct:

```
>>> george[mask | (george <= 2)]
1968    10
Name: George Songs, dtype: int64
```

Tip

If you inline boolean array operations, make sure to surround them with parentheses.

6.7 Summary

In this chapter, we looked at the index. Through index operations, we can pull values out of a series. Because you can pull out values by both position and label, indexing can be a little complicated. Using .loc and .iloc allow you to be more explicit about indexing operations. We can also use *slicing* to pull out values. This is a

33

6. Series Indexing

powerful construct that allows use to be succinct in our code. In addition, we can also use *boolean arrays* to filter data.

Note that the operations in this chapter also apply to `DataFrames`. In future chapters we will see their application. In the next chapter, we will examine some of the powerful methods that are built-in to the `Series` object.

Chapter 7

Series Methods

A `Series` object has many attributes and methods that are useful for data analysis. This section will cover a few of them.

In general, the methods return a new `Series` object. Most of the methods returning a new instance also have an `inplace` or a `copy` parameter. This is because the default behavior tends towards immutability, and these optional parameters default to `False` and `True` respectively.

> **Note**
>
> The `inplace` and `copy` parameters are the logical complement of each other. Luckily, a method will only take one of them. This is one of those slight inconsistencies found in the library. In practice, immutability works out well and both of these parameters can be ignored.

The examples in this chapter will use the following series. They contain the count of Beatles songs attributed to individual band members in the years 1966 and 1969:

```
>>> songs_66 = pd.Series([3, None , 11, 9],
...       index=['George', 'Ringo', 'John', 'Paul'],
...       name='Counts')
>>> songs_69 = pd.Series([18, 22, 7, 5],
...       index=[ 'John', 'Paul', 'George', 'Ringo'],
...       name='Counts')
```

7.1 Iteration

Iteration over a series iterates over the values:

7. Series Methods

```
>>> for value in songs_66:
...     print(value)
3.0
nan
11.0
9.0
```

There is an .iteritems method to loop over the index, value pairs:

```
>>> for idx, value in songs_66.iteritems():
...     print(idx, value)
George 3.0
Ringo nan
John 11.0
Paul 9.0
```

Note

Python supports *unpacking* or *destructuring* during variable assignment, which includes iteration (as seen in the example above). The .iteritems method returns a sequence of index, value tuples. By using unpacking, we can immediately put them each in their own variables.

If Python did not support this feature, we would have to create an intermediate variable to hold the tuple (which works but adds a few more lines of code):

```
>>> for items in songs_66.iteritems():
...     idx = items[0]
...     value = items[1]
...     print(idx, value)
George 3.0
Ringo nan
John 11.0
Paul 9.0
```

A .keys method is provided as a shortcut to the index as well:

```
>>> for idx in songs_66.keys():
...     print(idx)
George
Ringo
John
Paul
```

Unlike the .keys method of a Python dictionary, the result is ordered.

7.2 Overloaded operations

The table below lists *overloaded* operations for a `Series` object. The operations behave in a special way for pandas objects that might be different than other Python objects respond to these operations:

Operation	Result
+	Adds scalar (or series with matching index values) returns `Series`
-	Subtracts scalar (or series with matching index values) returns `Series`
/	Divides scalar (or series with matching index values) returns `Series`
//	"Floor" Divides scalar (or series with matching index values) returns `Series`
*	Multiplies scalar (or series with matching index values) returns `Series`
%	Modulus scalar (or series with matching index values) returns `Series`
==, !=	Equality scalar (or series with matching index values) returns `Series`
>, <	Greater/less than scalar (or series with matching index values) returns `Series`
>=, <=	Greater/less than or equal scalar (or series with matching index values) returns `Series`
^	Binary XOR returns `Series`
|	Binary OR returns `Series`
&	Binary AND returns `Series`

The common arithmetic operations for a series are overloaded to work with both scalars and other series objects. Addition with a scalar (assuming numeric values in the series) simply adds the scalar value to the values of the series. Adding a scalar to a series is called *broadcasting*:

```
>>> songs_66 + 2
George    5.0
Ringo     NaN
John      13.0
Paul      11.0
Name: Counts, dtype: float64
```

37

7. Series Methods

Note

Broadcasting is a NumPy and pandas feature. A normal Python list supports some of the operations listed in the prior table, but not in the elementwise manner that NumPy and pandas objects do. When you multiply a Python list by two, the result is a new list with the elements repeated, not each element multiplied by two:

```
>>> [1, 3, 4] * 2
[1, 3, 4, 1, 3, 4]
```

To multiply every element in a list by two using idiomatic Python, one would use a list comprehension:

```
>>> [x*2 for x in [1, 3, 4]]
[2, 6, 8]
```

Addition with two series objects adds only those items whose index occurs in both series, otherwise it inserts a NaN for index values found only in one of the series. Note that though Ringo appears in both indices, he has a value of NaN in songs_66 (leading to NaN as the result of the addition operation):

```
>>> songs_66 + songs_69
George    10.0
John      29.0
Paul      31.0
Ringo      NaN
Name: Counts, dtype: float64
```

Note

The above result might be problematic. Should the count of Ringo songs really be unknown? In this case, we use the fillna method to replace NaN with zero and give us a better answer:

```
>>> songs_66.fillna(0) + songs_69.fillna(0)
George    10.0
John      29.0
Paul      31.0
Ringo      5.0
Name: Counts, dtype: float64
```

The other arithmetic operations behave similarly for -, *, and /. Multiplying song counts for two years really doesn't make sense, but pandas supports it:

7.3. Getting and Setting Values

```
>>> songs_66 - songs_69
George    -4.0
John      -7.0
Paul     -13.0
Ringo      NaN
Name: Counts, dtype: float64

>>> songs_66 * songs_69
George    21.0
John     198.0
Paul     198.0
Ringo      NaN
Name: Counts, dtype: float64
```

7.3 Getting and Setting Values

The series object allows for access to values by index operations (with .loc and .iloc) and convenience methods. The methods for getting and setting values at index labels are listed in the table below:

Method	Result
get(label, [default])	Returns a scalar (or Series if duplicate indexes) for label or default on failed lookup.
get_value(label)	Returns a scalar (or Series if duplicate indexes) for label
set_value(label, value)	Returns a new Series with label and value inserted (or updated)

Let's examine getting and setting data with both operations:

```
>>> songs_66
George    3.0
Ringo     NaN
John     11.0
Paul      9.0
Name: Counts, dtype: float64

>>> songs_66['John']
11.0

>>> songs_66.get_value('John')
11.0
```

There is another trick up pandas' sleeve. It supports dotted attribute access for index names that are valid attribute names (and don't conflict with pre-existing series attributes):

```
>>> songs_66.John
11.0
```

39

7. Series Methods

Note

Valid attribute names are names that begin with letters, and contain alphanumerics or underscores. If an index name contains spaces, you couldn't use dotted attribute access to read it, but index access would work fine:

```
>>> songs_lastname = pd.Series([3, 11],
...        index=['George H', 'John L'])

>>> songs_lastname.George H
Traceback (most recent call last):
   ...
   songs_lastname.George H
                        ^
SyntaxError: invalid syntax

>>> songs_lastname['George H']
3
```

If an index name conflicts with an existing series method or attribute, dotted access fails:

```
>>> nums = pd.Series([4, 10],
...        index=['count', 'median'])

>>> nums.count
<bound method Series.count of count     4
median    10
dtype: int64>

>>> nums['count']
4
```

Dotted attribute access is a handy shortcut to eliminate a few keystrokes, but if your aren't careful, you might get unexpected results. Index operations, on the other hand, should always work.

As a convenience, .get (similar to .get on a native Python dictionary) is provided. It provides an optional parameter to return should the lookup fail:

```
>>> songs_66.get('Fred', 'missing')
'missing'
```

The .get_value method raises an exception if the index value is missing:

```
>>> songs_66.get_value('Fred')
Traceback (most recent call last):
   ...
KeyError: 'Fred'
```

40

7.3. Getting and Setting Values

There are various mechanisms to perform assignment on a pandas series. Assignment that occurs with .__setitem__ *updates the series in place*, but does not return a series:

```
>>> songs_66['John'] = 82
>>> songs_66['John']
82.0
```

Dotted attribute setting works as well, given a valid attribute name:

```
>>> songs_66.John = 81
>>> songs_66.John
81.0
```

Note

The Python language gives you great flexibility. But with that flexibility comes responsibility. Paraphrasing Spiderman here, but because dotted attribute setting is possible, one can overwrite some of the methods and attributes of a series.

Below is a series that has various index names. normal is a perfectly valid name. median is a fine name, but is also the name of the method for calculating the median. class is another name that would be fine if wasn't a reserved name in Python. The final is the name of series attribute that pandas tries to protect:

```
>>> ser = pd.Series([1, 2, 3, 4],
...      index=['normal', 'median', 'class', 'index'])
```

We can overwrite the first two index names:

```
>>> ser.normal = 4
>>> ser.median = 5
```

But trying to overwrite the reserved word throws an error:

```
>>> ser.class = 6
Traceback (most recent call last):
  ...
    ser.class = 6
        ^
SyntaxError: invalid syntax
```

Setting the index index also fails:

```
>>> ser.index = 7
Traceback (most recent call last):
  ...
TypeError: Index(...) must be called with a collection of
```

41

7. Series Methods

```
some kind, 7 was passed
```

When you go back to access the values you might be surprised. Only normal was updated. The write to 'median silently failed:

```
>>> ser
normal   4
median   2
class    3
index    4
dtype: int64
```

My recommendation is to stay away from dotted attribute setting.

If you are new to Python and not familiar with the keywords, the module keyword has a `kwlist` attribute. This attribute is a list containing all the current keywords for Python:

```
>>> import keyword
>>> print(keyword.kwlist)
['False', 'None', 'True', 'and',
'as', 'assert', 'break', 'class',
'continue', 'def', 'del', 'elif',
'else', 'except', 'finally', 'for',
'from', 'global', 'if', 'import',
'in', 'is', 'lambda', 'nonlocal',
'not', 'or', 'pass', 'raise',
'return', 'try', 'while', 'with',
'yield']
```

The `.set_value` method updates the series in place *and returns a series*:

```
>>> songs_66.set_value('John', 80)
George     3.0
Ringo      NaN
John      80.0
Paul       9.0
Name: Counts, dtype: float64

>>> songs_66['John']
80.0
```

Also, `.set_value` will update all the values for a given index. If you have non-unique indexes and only want to update one of the values for a repeated index, this cannot be done via `.set_value`.

Tip

One way to update only one value for a repeated index label is to update by position. The following series repeats the index label 1970:

```
>>> george = pd.Series([10, 7, 1, 22],
...     index=['1968', '1969', '1970', '1970'],
...     name='George Songs')
>>> george
1968    10
1969     7
1970     1
1970    22
Name: George Songs, dtype: int64
```

To update only the first value for 1970, use the .iloc index assignment:

```
>>> george.iloc[2] = 3
>>> george
1968    10
1969     7
1970     3
1970    22
Name: George Songs, dtype: int64
```

A quick method of to retrieve the index positions for values is to use a list comprehension on the .iteritems method in combination with the built-in enumerate function:

```
>>> [pos for pos, x in enumerate(george.iteritems()) \
...     if x[0] == '1970']
[2, 3]
```

7.4 Reset Index

Because selection, plotting, joining, and other methods can be determined by the index, often it is useful to change the values of the index. We will examine a few of the methods to reset the index, change which index labels are present, and rename the labels of the index. The first, .reset_index, will reset the index to monotonically increasing integers starting from zero. By default, the .reset_index method will return a new data frame (not a series). It moves the current index values to a column named index:

```
>>> songs_66.reset_index()
    index  Counts
0  George     3.0
1   Ringo     NaN
2    John    80.0
3    Paul     9.0
```

43

7. Series Methods

To get a series out, pass True to the drop parameter, which will drop the index column:

```
>>> songs_66.reset_index(drop=True)
0     3.0
1     NaN
2    80.0
3     9.0
Name: Counts, dtype: float64
```

If a specific index order is desired, it may be passed to the .reindex method. The index of the result will be conformed to the index passed in. New index values will have a value of the optional parameter fill_value (which defaults to NaN):

```
>>> songs_66.reindex(['Billy', 'Eric', 'George', 'Yoko'])
Billy     NaN
Eric      NaN
George    3.0
Yoko      NaN
Name: Counts, dtype: float64
```

Alternatively, the values of the index can be updated with the .rename method. This method accepts either a dictionary mapping index labels to new labels, or a function that accepts a label and returns a new one:

```
>>> songs_66.rename({'Ringo':'Richard'})
George      3.0
Richard     NaN
John       80.0
Paul        9.0
Name: Counts, dtype: float64
```

```
>>> songs_66.rename(lambda x: x.lower())
george     3.0
ringo      NaN
john      80.0
paul       9.0
Name: Counts, dtype: float64
```

As a poor-man's solution, the index attribute can be changed under the covers. This works as well, and pandas will convert a list into an actual Index object. The problem with such interactions is that it is treating the series as mutable, when most methods do not. In the author's opinion, it is safer to use the methods described above:

```
>>> idx = songs_66.index
>>> idx
Index(['George', 'Ringo', 'John', 'Paul'], dtype='object')

>>> idx2 = range(len(idx))
```

44

7.5. Counts

```
>>> list(idx2)
[0, 1, 2, 3]
>>> songs_66.index = idx2
>>> songs_66
0     3.0
1     NaN
2    80.0
3     9.0
Name: Counts, dtype: float64

>>> songs_66.index
RangeIndex(start=0, stop=4, step=1)
```

Note

The above code explicitly calls the list function on idx2 because the author is using Python 3 in the examples in this book. In Python 3, range is an *iterable* that does not materialize the contents of the sequence until it is iterated over. It behaves similar to Python 2's xrange built-in.

This code (as with most of the code in this book) will still work in Python 2.

7.5 Counts

This section will explore how to get an overview of the data found in a series. For the following examples we will use two series. The songs_66 series:

```
>>> songs_66 = pd.Series([3, None , 11, 9],
...      index=['George', 'Ringo', 'John', 'Paul'],
...      name='Counts')

>>> songs_66
George     3.0
Ringo      NaN
John      11.0
Paul       9.0
Name: Counts, dtype: float64
```

And the scores_2 series:

```
>>> scores2 = pd.Series([67.3, 100, 96.7, None, 100],
...      index=['Ringo', 'Paul', 'George', 'Peter', 'Billy'],
...      name='test2')

>>> scores2
Ringo      67.3
Paul      100.0
George     96.7
Peter       NaN
Billy     100.0
```

45

7. Series Methods

```
Name: test2, dtype: float64
```

A few methods are provided to get a feel for the counts of the entries, how many are unique, and how many are duplicated. Given a series, the .count method returns the number of non-null items. The scores2 series has 5 entries but one of them is None, so .count only returns 4:

```
>>> scores2.count()
4
```

Histogram tables are easy to generate in pandas. The .value_counts method returns a series indexed by the values found in the series. If you think of a series as an ordered mapping of index keys to values, .value_counts returns a mapping of those values to their counts, ordered by frequency:

```
>>> scores2.value_counts()
100.0    2
67.3     1
96.7     1
Name: test2, dtype: int64
```

To get the unique values or the count of non-NaN items use the .unique and .nunique methods respectively. Note that .unique includes the nan value, but .nunique does not count it:

```
>>> scores2.unique()
array([ 67.3,  100. ,   96.7,    nan])
>>> scores2.nunique()
3
```

Dealing with duplicate values is another feature of pandas. To drop duplicate values use the .drop_duplicates method. Since Billy has the same score as Paul, he will get dropped:

```
>>> scores2.drop_duplicates()
Ringo     67.3
Paul     100.0
George    96.7
Peter      NaN
Name: test2, dtype: float64
```

To retrieve a series with boolean values indicating whether its value was repeated, use the .duplicated method:

```
>>> scores2.duplicated()
Ringo    False
Paul     False
George   False
Peter    False
Billy     True
Name: test2, dtype: bool
```

To drop duplicate index entries requires a little more effort. Lets create a series, scores3, that has 'Paul' in the index twice. If we use the .groupby method, and group by the index, we can then take the first or last item from the values for each index label:

```
>>> scores3 = pd.Series([67.3, 100, 96.7, None, 100, 79],
...      index=['Ringo', 'Paul', 'George', 'Peter', 'Billy',
...      'Paul'])
>>> scores3.groupby(scores3.index).first()
Billy    100.0
George    96.7
Paul     100.0
Peter      NaN
Ringo     67.3
dtype: float64

>>> scores3.groupby(scores3.index).last()
Billy    100.0
George    96.7
Paul      79.0
Peter      NaN
Ringo     67.3
dtype: float64
```

7.6 Statistics

There are many basic statistical measures in a series object's methods. We will look at a few of them in this section.

One of the most basic measurements is the sum of the values in a series:

```
>>> songs_66.sum()
23.0
```

Note

Most of the methods that perform a calculation ignore NaN. Some also provide an optional parameter—skipna—to change that behavior. But in practice if you do not ignore NaN, the result is nan:

```
>>> songs_66.sum(skipna=False)
nan
```

Calculating the *mean* (the "expected value" or average) and the *median* (the "middle" value at 50% that separates the lower values from the upper values) is simple. As discussed, both of these methods ignore NaN (unless skipna is set to False):

7. Series Methods

```
>>> songs_66.mean()
7.666666666666667

>>> songs_66.median()
9.0
```

For non-normal distributions, the median is useful as a summary measure. It is more resilient to outliers. In addition, *quantile* measures can be used to predict the 50% value (the default) or any level desired, such as the 10th and 90th percentile. The default quantile calculation should be very similar to the median:

```
>>> songs_66.quantile()
9.0

>>> songs_66.quantile(.1)
4.2000000000000002

>>> songs_66.quantile(.9)
10.6
```

To get a good overall feel for the series, the .describe method presents a good number of summary statistics and returns the result as a series. It includes the count of values, their mean, standard deviation, minimum and maximum values, and the 25%, 50%, and 75% quantiles:

```
>>> songs_66.describe()
count     3.000000
mean      7.666667
std       4.163332
min       3.000000
25%       6.000000
50%       9.000000
75%      10.000000
max      11.000000
Name: Counts, dtype: float64
```

You can pass in specific percentiles if you so desire with the percentiles parameter:

```
>>> songs_66.describe(percentiles=[.05, .1, .2])
count     3.000000
mean      7.666667
std       4.163332
min       3.000000
5%        3.600000
10%       4.200000
20%       5.400000
50%       9.000000
max      11.000000
Name: Counts, dtype: float64
```

The series also has methods to find the minimum and maximum for the values, .min and .max. In addition, there are methods to

7.6. Statistics

get the index location of the minimum and maximum index labels, .idxmin and .idxmax:

```
>>> songs_66.min()
3.0

>>> songs_66.idxmin()
'George'

>>> songs_66.max()
11.0

>>> songs_66.idxmax()
'John'
```

The rest of this section briefly lists other statistical measures. Wikipedia is a great resource for a more thorough explanation of these. As statisticians tend to be precise, the articles found there are well curated.

Though the minimum and maximum are interesting values, often they are outliers. In that case, it is useful to find the spread of the values taking into account the notion of outliers. *Variance* is one of these measures. A low variance indicates that most of the values are close to the mean:

```
>>> songs_66.var()
17.333333333333329
```

The square root of the variance is known as the *standard deviation*. This is also a common measure to indicate spread from the mean. In a normal distribution, 99% of the values will be within three standard deviations above and below the mean:

```
>>> songs_66.std()
4.1633319989322652
```

Another summary statistic for describing dispersion is the *mean absolute deviation*. In pandas this is calculated by averaging the absolute values of the difference between the mean and the values:

```
>>> songs_66.mad()
3.1111111111111107
```

Skew is a summary statistic that measures how the tails behave. A normal distribution should have a skew around 0. A negative skew indicates that the left tail is longer, whereas a positive skew indicates that the right tail is longer. Below is a plot of the histogram:

```
>>> import matplotlib.pyplot as plt
>>> fig = plt.figure()
>>> ax = fig.add_subplot(111)
>>> songs_66.hist(ax=ax)
>>> fig.savefig('/tmp/song-hist.png')
```

7. Series Methods

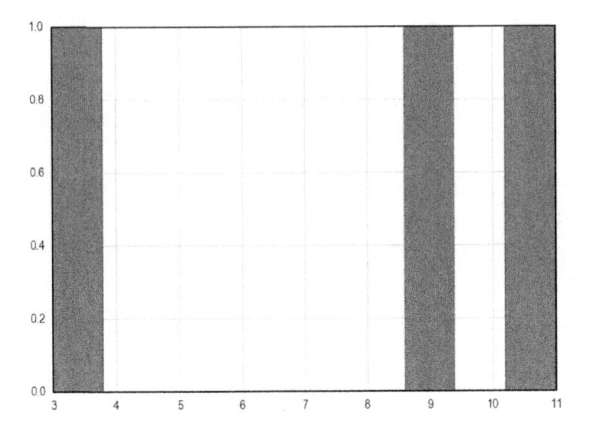

Figure 7.1: A histogram that illustrates negative skew

In this case the sample size is so low that it is hard to say much about the data. But the numbers say a negative skew:

```
>>> songs_66.skew()
-1.293342780733397
```

Kurtosis is a summary measure that describes how narrow the "peak" of is distribution is. The larger the number, the narrower the peak is. Normally, this value is reported alongside skew. The .kurt method returns nan if there are fewer than four numbers:

```
>>> songs_66.kurt()
nan
```

Covariance is a measure of how two variables change together. If they tend to increase together, it will be positive. If one tends to decrease while the other increases, it will be negative:

```
>>> songs_66.cov(songs_69)
28.333333333333332
```

When the covariance is normalized (by dividing by the standard deviations of both series), it is called the correlation coefficient. The .corr method gives the *Pearson Correlation Coefficient*. This value is a number from -1 to 1. The more positive this value is, the greater the correlation. The more negative it is, the greater the inverse correlation. A value of zero indicates no correlation:

7.6. Statistics

```
>>> songs_66.corr(songs_69)
0.87614899364978038
```

The *autocorrelation* measure describes the correlation of a series with itself shifted one position. 1 indicates perfect correlation, and -1 indicates anti-correlation. Here is another case where the sample size is small, so take these with a grain of salt. Note that .autocorr does not ignore NaN by default:

```
>>> songs_66.autocorr()
nan

>>> songs_66.dropna().autocorr()
-0.99999999999999989
```

The first discrete difference of a series is available as well:

```
>>> songs_66.diff()
George    NaN
Ringo     NaN
John      NaN
Paul     -2.0
Name: Counts, dtype: float64
```

Often, the cumulative sum of a series is needed. The .cumsum method provides this. In addition, there are analogous operations for cumulative product and cumulative minimum:

```
>>> songs_66.cumsum()
George     3.0
Ringo      NaN
John      14.0
Paul      23.0
Name: Counts, dtype: float64

>>> songs_66.cumprod()
George     3.0
Ringo      NaN
John      33.0
Paul     297.0
Name: Counts, dtype: float64

>>> songs_66.cummin()
George     3.0
Ringo      NaN
John       3.0
Paul       3.0
Name: Counts, dtype: float64
```

7. Series Methods

7.7 Convert Types

The series object has the ability to tweak its values. The numerical values in a series may be rounded up to the next whole floating point number by using the .round method:

```
>>> songs_66.round()
George    3.0
Ringo     NaN
John      11.0
Paul      9.0
Name: Counts, dtype: float64
```

Note that even though the value is rounded, the type is still a float.

Numbers can be clipped between lower and upper thresholds using the .clip method. This method does not change the type either:

```
>>> songs_66.clip(lower=80, upper=90)
George    80.0
Ringo     NaN
John      80.0
Paul      80.0
Name: Counts, dtype: float64
```

The .astype method attempts to convert values to the type passed in. In the instance below, the float values are being converted to strings. To the unwary, there does not appear to be much change other than the dtype changing to object:

```
>>> songs_66.astype(str)
George    3.0
Ringo
John      11.0
Paul      9.0
Name: Counts, dtype: object
```

But, if a method is invoked on the converted string values, the result might not be the desired output. In this case .max now returns the lexicographic maximum:

```
>>> songs_66.astype(str).max()
'nan'
```

There is also a .convert_objects method in pandas that behaves similarly to .astype, but it has been deprecated, as of version 0.17. The current recommendation for type conversion is to use the following methods:

52

7.8. Dealing with None

Final Type	Method
string	use `.astype(str)`
numeric	use `pd.to_numeric`
integer	use `.astype(int)`, note that this will fail with NaN
datetime	use `pd.to_datetime`

By default, the `to_*` functions will raise an error if they cannot coerce. In the case below, the `to_numeric` function cannot convert nan to a float. This is slightly annoying:

```
>>> pd.to_numeric(songs_66.apply(str))
Traceback (most recent call last):
  ...
ValueError: Unable to parse string
```

Luckily, the `to_numeric` function has an `errors` parameter, that when passed `'coerce'` will fill in with NaN if it cannot coerce:

```
>>> pd.to_numeric(songs_66.astype(str), errors='coerce')
George    3.0
Ringo     NaN
John     11.0
Paul      9.0
Name: Counts, dtype: float64
```

The `to_datetime` function also behaves similarly, and also raises errors when it fails to coerce:

```
>>> pd.to_datetime(pd.Series(['Sep 7, 2001',
...     '9/8/2001', '9-9-2001', '10th of September 2001',
...     'Once de Septiembre 2001']))
Traceback (most recent call last):
  ...
ValueError: Unknown string format
```

If we pass `errors='coerce'`, we can see that it supports many formats if, but not Spanish:

```
>>> pd.to_datetime(pd.Series(['Sep 7, 2001',
...     '9/8/2001', '9-9-2001', '10th of September 2001',
...     'Once de Septiembre 2001']), errors='coerce')
0   2001-09-07
1   2001-09-08
2   2001-09-09
3   2001-09-10
4          NaT
dtype: datetime64[ns]
```

7.8 Dealing with None

As mentioned previously, the NaN value is usually disregarded in calculations. Sometimes, it is useful to fill them in with another

7. Series Methods

value. The .fillna method will replace them with a given value, -1 in this case:

```
>>> songs_66.fillna(-1)
George     3.0
Ringo     -1.0
John      11.0
Paul       9.0
Name: Counts, dtype: float64
```

NaN values can be dropped from the series using .dropna:

```
>>> songs_66.dropna()
George     3.0
John      11.0
Paul       9.0
Name: Counts, dtype: float64
```

Another way to get the non-NaN values (or the complement) is to create a boolean array of the values that are not NaN. With this array in hand, we can use it to mask the series. The .notnull method gives us this boolean array:

```
>>> val_mask = songs_66.notnull()

>>> val_mask
George    True
Ringo     False
John      True
Paul      True
Name: Counts, dtype: bool

>>> songs_66[val_mask]
George     3.0
John      11.0
Paul       9.0
Name: Counts, dtype: float64
```

If we want the mask for the NaN positions, we can use .isnull:

```
>>> nan_mask = songs_66.isnull()

>>> nan_mask
George    False
Ringo     True
John      False
Paul      False
Name: Counts, dtype: bool

>>> songs_66[nan_mask]
Ringo    NaN
Name: Counts, dtype: float64
```

Note

We can flip a boolean mask by applying the not operator (~):

```
>>> ~nan_mask
George    True
Ringo     False
John      True
Paul      True
Name: Counts, dtype: bool
```

So, `songs_66.isnull()` is equivalent to `~songs_66.notnull()`.

Locating the position of the first and last valid index values is simple as well, using the `.first_valid_index` and `.last_valid_index` methods respectively:

```
>>> songs_66.first_valid_index()
'George'

>>> songs_66.last_valid_index()
'Paul'
```

7.9 Matrix Operations

Computing the dot product is available through the `.dot` method. But, this method fails if NaN is part of the series:

```
>>> songs_66.dot(songs_69)
nan
```

Removing NaN will give a value for `.dot`:

```
>>> songs_66.dropna().dot(songs_66.dropna())
211.0
```

A series also has a `.transpose` method (alternatively invoked as the T property) that is actually a no-op and just returns the series. (In the two dimensional data frame, the columns and rows are transposed):

```
>>> songs_66.T
George    3.0
Ringo     NaN
John      11.0
Paul      9.0
Name: Counts, dtype: float64

>>> songs_66.transpose()
George    3.0
Ringo     NaN
John      11.0
```

7. SERIES METHODS

```
Paul       9.0
Name: Counts, dtype: float64
```

7.10 Append, combining, and joining two series

To concatenate two series together, simply use the .append method. Unlike the .append method of a Python list which takes a single item to be appended to the list, this method takes another Series object as its' parameter:

```
>>> songs_66.append(songs_69)
George     3.0
Ringo      NaN
John       11.0
Paul       9.0
John       18.0
Paul       22.0
George     7.0
Ringo      5.0
Name: Counts, dtype: float64
```

The .append method will create duplicate indexes by default (as seen by the multiple entries for Paul above). .append has an optional parameter, verify_integrity, which when set to True to complain if index values are duplicated:

```
>>> songs_66.append(songs_69, verify_integrity=True)
Traceback (most recent call last):
  ...
ValueError: Indexes have overlapping values: ['George',
'John', 'Paul', 'Ringo']
```

To perform element-wise operations on series, use the .combine method. It takes another series, and a function as its' parameters. The function should accept two parameters and perform a reduction on them. Below is one way to compute the average of two series using .combine:

```
>>> def avg(v1, v2):
...     return (v1 + v2)/2.0

>>> songs_66.combine(songs_69, avg)
George     5.0
John       14.5
Paul       15.5
Ringo      NaN
Name: Counts, dtype: float64
```

To update values from one series, use the .update method. It accepts a new series and will return a series that has replaced the values using the passed in series:

7.11. Sorting

```
>>> songs_66.update(songs_69)
>>> songs_66
George     7.0
Ringo      5.0
John      18.0
Paul      22.0
Name: Counts, dtype: float64
```

Note

.update is another method that is an anomaly from most other pandas methods. It behaves similarly to the .update method of a native Python dictionary—it *does not return anything* and *updates the values in place*. Tread with caution.

The .repeat method simply repeats every item a desired amount:

```
>>> songs_69.repeat(2)
John      18
John      18
Paul      22
Paul      22
George     7
George     7
Ringo      5
Ringo      5
Name: Counts, dtype: int64
```

7.11 Sorting

There are various methods for sorting that we will examine. Be careful with the .sort method. This method provides an in-place sort based on the values. If you are merrily programming along, and re-assigning the series object with each method invocation (due to the general immutability of Series), this will fail. This method has no return value, and is provided to have some compatibility with NumPy:

```
>>> songs_66
George     7.0
Ringo      5.0
John      18.0
Paul      22.0
Name: Counts, dtype: float64

>>> orig = songs_66.copy()

>>> songs_66.sort()
>>> songs_66
Ringo      5.0
```

7. Series Methods

```
George    7.0
John     18.0
Paul     22.0
Name: Counts, dtype: float64
```

As the .sort method behaves differently from most pandas methods, it has been deprecated in version 0.17. The suggested replacement is the .sort_values method. That method returns a new series:

```
>>> orig.sort_values()
Ringo     5.0
George    7.0
John     18.0
Paul     22.0
Name: Counts, dtype: float64
```

Note

The .sort_values exposes a kind parameter. The default value is 'quicksort', which is generally fast. Another option to pass to kind is 'mergesort'. When this is passed, .sort_values performs a *stable sort* (so that items that sort in the same position will not move relative to one another) when this method is invoked. Here's a small example:

```
>>> s = pd.Series([2, 2, 2], index=['a2', 'a1', 'a3'])
```

Note that a *mergesort* does not re-arrange items that are already ordered correctly (in this case everything is already ordered):

```
>>> s.sort_values(kind='mergesort')
a2    2
a1    2
a3    2
dtype: int64
```

Other sorting kinds might re-order rows (see that a2 is moved to the bottom in this heapsort example):

```
>>> s.sort_values(kind='heapsort')
a1    2
a3    2
a2    2
dtype: int64
```

Note that it is possible that a heapsort (or any non-mergesort) might not re-arrange the ordered rows, but consider this luck, and don't rely on that behavior if you need a stable sort.

7.12. Applying a function

This .sort_values method also supports the ascending parameter that flips the order of the sort:

```
>>> songs_66.sort_values(ascending=False)
Paul      22.0
John      18.0
George     7.0
Ringo      5.0
Name: Counts, dtype: float64
```

Note

The .order method in pandas is similar to .sort and .sort_values. It is deprecated as of 0.18, so please use .sort_values instead.

The .sort_index method does not operate in place and returns a new series. It has an optional parameter, ascending that will reverse the index if desired:

```
>>> songs_66.sort_index()
George     7.0
John      18.0
Paul      22.0
Ringo      5.0
Name: Counts, dtype: float64
>>> songs_66.sort_index(ascending=False)
Ringo      5.0
Paul      22.0
John      18.0
George     7.0
Name: Counts, dtype: float64
```

Another useful sorting related method is .rank. This method ranks the index by the values of the entries. It assigns equal weights for ties. It also supports the ascending parameter to reverse the order:

```
>>> songs_66.rank()
Ringo     1.0
George    2.0
John      3.0
Paul      4.0
Name: Counts, dtype: float64
```

7.12 Applying a function

Often the values in a series will need to be altered, cleaned up, checked, or have an arbitrary function applied to them. The .map method applies a function to every item in the series. Below is a

7. Series Methods

function, format, that creates a string that appends song or songs to the number depending on the count:

```
>>> def format(x):
...     if x == 1:
...         template = '{} song'
...     else:
...         template = '{} songs'
...     return template.format(x)

>>> songs_66.map(format)
Ringo       5.0 songs
George      7.0 songs
John       18.0 songs
Paul       22.0 songs
Name: Counts, dtype: object
```

In addition to accepting a function, the .map function also accepts a dictionary. In that case, any value of the series matching a key in the dictionary will be updated to the corresponding value for the key:

```
>>> songs_66.map({5: None,
...               18.: 21,
...               22.: 23})
Ringo     NaN
George    NaN
John      21.0
Paul      23.0
Name: Counts, dtype: float64
```

Similarly, the .map will accept a series, treating it much like a dictionary. Any value of the series that matches the passed in index value will be updated to the corresponding value:

```
>>> mapping = pd.Series({22.: 33})
>>> mapping
22.0    33
dtype: int64

>>> songs_66.map(mapping)
Ringo     NaN
George    NaN
John      NaN
Paul      33.0
Name: Counts, dtype: float64
```

There is also an .apply method on the series object. It behaves very similar to .map, but it only works with functions (not with series nor dictionaries).

7.13 Serialization

We have seen examples that create a Series object from a list, a dictionary, or another series. In addition, a series will serialize to and from a CSV file.

To save a series as a CSV file, simply pass a file object to the .to_csv method. The following example shows how this is done with a StringIO object (it implements the file interface, but allows us to easily inspect the results):

```
>>> from io import StringIO
>>> fout = StringIO()
>>> songs_66.to_csv(fout)
>>> print(fout.getvalue())
Ringo,5.0
George,7.0
John,18.0
Paul,22.0
```

Note

Some of the intentions of Python 3 were to make things consistent and clean up warts or annoyances in Python 2. Python 3 created an io module to handle reading and writing from streams. In Python 2 the import above should be:

```
>>> from StringIO import StringIO
```

To use a real file, the current best practice in Python is to use a *context manager*. This will automatically close the file for you when the indented block exits:

```
>>> with open('/tmp/songs_66.csv', 'w') as fout:
...     songs_66.to_csv(fout)
```

Upon closer examination of the serialized output, we see that the headers are missing. Pass in the header=True parameter to include headers in the output:

```
>>> fout = StringIO()
>>> songs_66.to_csv(fout, header=True)
>>> print(fout.getvalue())
,Counts
Ringo,5.0
George,7.0
John,18.0
Paul,22.0
```

As shown above, now the label for the index is missing. To remedy that, use the index_label parameter:

61

7. Series Methods

```
>>> fout = StringIO()
>>> songs_66.to_csv(fout, header=True, index_label='Name')
>>> print(fout.getvalue())
Name,Counts
Ringo,5.0
George,7.0
John,18.0
Paul,22.0
```

Note

The name of the series must be specified for the header of the values to appear. This can be passed in as a parameter during creation. Alternatively you can set the .name attribute of the series.

Below is a buggy attempt to create a series from a CSV file, using the .from_csv method:

```
>>> fout.seek(0)
>>> series = pd.Series.from_csv(fout)
>>> series
Name       Counts
Ringo       5.0
George      7.0
John       18.0
Paul       22.0
dtype: object
```

In this case, the values of the series are strings (notice the dtype: object). This is because the header was parsed as a value, and not as a header. The pandas parsing code was not able to coerce test2 into a numerical value, and assumed the column had string values. Here is a second attempt that reads it the data as numerics and uses line zero as the header:

```
>>> fout.seek(0)
>>> series = pd.Series.from_csv(fout, header=0)
>>> series
Name
Ringo       5.0
George      7.0
John       18.0
Paul       22.0
Name: Counts, dtype: float64
```

Note that the .name attribute is recovered as well:

```
>>> series.name
'Counts'
```

62

Note

In practice, when dealing with data frames, the read_csv function is used, rather than invoking the .from_csv classmethod on Series or DataFrame. The result of this function is a DataFrame rather than a Series:

```
>>> fout.seek(0)
>>> df = pd.read_csv(fout, index_col=0)
>>> df
        Counts
Name
Ringo      5.0
George     7.0
John      18.0
Paul      22.0
```

We can pull the Counts column out of the df data frame to create a Series. The Counts column contains floats now as the read_csv function expects header columns by default (unlike the series method), and tries to figure out types:

```
>>> df['Counts']
Name
Ringo      5.0
George     7.0
John      18.0
Paul      22.0
Name: Counts, dtype: float64
```

7.14 String operations

A series that has string data can be manipulated by *vectorized string operations*. Though it is possible to accomplish these same operations via the .map or .apply methods, prudent users will first look to see if a built-in method is provided. Typically, built-in methods will be faster because they are vectorized and often implemented in Cython, so there is less overhead. Using .map and .apply should be thought of as a last resort, instead of the first tool you reach for.

To invoke the string operations, simply invoke them on the .str attribute of the series:

```
>>> names = pd.Series(['George', 'John', 'Paul'])
>>> names.str.lower()
0    george
1    john
2    paul
dtype: object

>>> names.str.findall('o')
0    [o]
```

7. Series Methods

```
1     [o]
2     []
dtype: object
```

As noted, the previous operations are also possible using the .apply method, though the vectorized operations are faster:

```
>>> def lower(val):
...     return val.lower()
>>> names.apply(lower)
0    george
1    john
2    paul
dtype: object
```

The following vectorized string methods are available and should be familiar to anyone with experience with the methods of native Python strings:

Method	Result
cat	Concatenate list of strings onto items
center	Centers strings to width
contains	Boolean for whether pattern matches
count	Count pattern occurs in string
decode	Decode a codec encoding
encode	Encode a codec encoding
endswith	Boolean if strings end with item
findall	Find pattern in string
get	Attribute access on items
join	Join items with separator
len	Return length of items
lower	Lowercase the items
lstrip	Remove whitespace on left of items
match	Find groups in items from the pattern
pad	Pad the items
repeat	Repeat the string a certain number of times
replace	Replace a pattern with a new value
rstrip	Remove whitespace on the right of items
slice	Pull out slices from strings
split	Split items by pattern
startswith	Boolean if strings starts with item
strip	Remove whitespace from the items
title	Titlecase the items
upper	Uppercase the items

7.15 Summary

This has been a long chapter. That is because there are a lot of methods on the Series object. We have looked at looping over the

7.15. Summary

values, overloaded operations, accessing values, changing the index, basics stats, coercion, dealing with missing values and more. You should have a good understanding of the power of the Series. In the next chapter, we will look at how to plot with a Series.

Chapter 8

Series Plotting

The `Series` object has a lot of built-in functionality. In addition to the rich functionality previously mentioned, they also have the ability to create plots using integration with matplotlib[9].

For this section, we will use the following values for `songs_69`:

```
>>> songs_69.name = 'Counts 69'
>>> songs_69
John      18
Paul      22
George     7
Ringo      5
Name: Counts 69, dtype: int64
```

And these values for `songs_66`:

```
>>> songs_66.name = 'Counts 66'
>>> songs_66['Eric'] = float('nan')
>>> songs_66
Ringo     5.0
George    7.0
John     18.0
Paul     22.0
Eric      NaN
Name: Counts 66, dtype: float64
```

Note that the index values have some overlap and that there is a NaN value as well.

The .plot method plots the index against value. If you are running from IPython or an interpreter, a matplotlib plot will appear when calling that method. In this case of the examples in the book, we are saving the plot as a png file which requires a bit more boilerplate. (The `matplotlib.pyplot` library needs to be loaded and

---

[9] matplotlib (http://matplotlib.org/) also refers to itself in lowercase.

67

8. Series Plotting

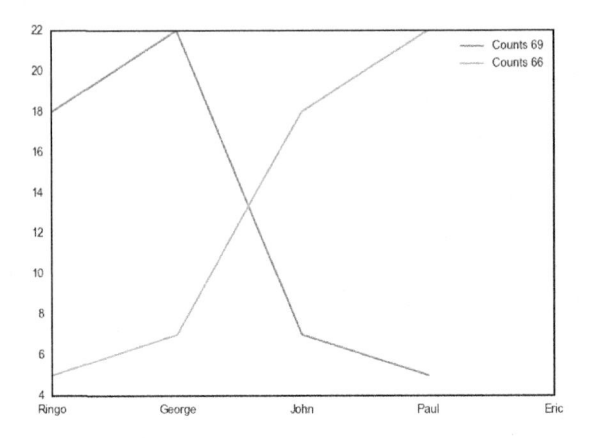

[Figure: line plot with x-axis labels Ringo, George, John, Paul, Eric and y-axis from 4 to 22, showing two series "Counts 69" and "Counts 66"]

Figure 8.1: Plotting two series that have string indexes. The default plot type is a line plot.

a Figure object needs to be created (plt.figure()) so we can call the .savefig method on it.)

Below is the code that shows default plots for both of the series. The call to plt.legend() will insert a legend in the plot. The code also saves the graph as a png file:

```
>>> import matplotlib.pyplot as plt
>>> fig = plt.figure()
>>> songs_69.plot()
>>> songs_66.plot()
>>> plt.legend()
>>> fig.savefig('/tmp/ex1.png')
```

By default, .plot creates line charts, but it can also create bar charts by changing the kind parameter. The bar chart is not stacked by default, so the bars will occlude one another. We address this in the example below by setting color for scores2 to black ('k') and lowering the transparency by setting the alpha parameter:

```
>>> fig = plt.figure()
>>> songs_69.plot(kind='bar')
>>> songs_66.plot(kind='bar', color='k', alpha=.5)
>>> plt.legend()
>>> fig.savefig('/tmp/ex2.png')
```

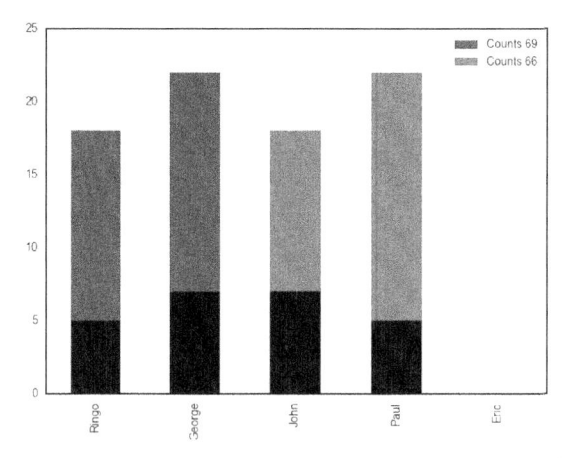

Figure 8.2: Plotting two series that have string indexes as bar plots.

We can also create histograms in pandas. First, we will create a series with a little more data in it, to make the histogram slightly more interesting:

```
>>> data = pd.Series(np.random.randn(500),
...                  name='500 random')
```

Creating the histogram is easy, we simply invoke the .hist method of the series:

```
>>> fig = plt.figure()
>>> ax = fig.add_subplot(111)
>>> data.hist()
>>> fig.savefig('/tmp/ex3.png')
```

This looks very similar to a matplotlib histogram:

```
>>> fig = plt.figure()
>>> ax = fig.add_subplot(111)
>>> ax.hist(data)
>>> fig.savefig('/tmp/ex3-1.png')
```

If we have installed scipy.stats, we can plot a kernel density estimation (KDE) plot. This plot is very similar to a histogram, but rather than using bins to represent areas where numbers fall, it plots a curved line:

```
>>> fig = plt.figure()
>>> data.plot(kind='kde')    # requires scipy.stats
```

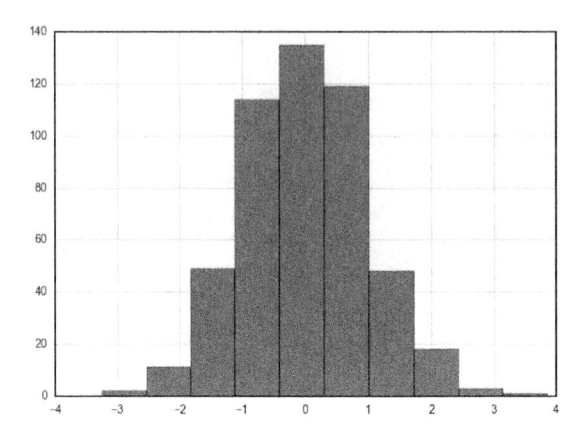

Figure 8.3: A pandas histogram.

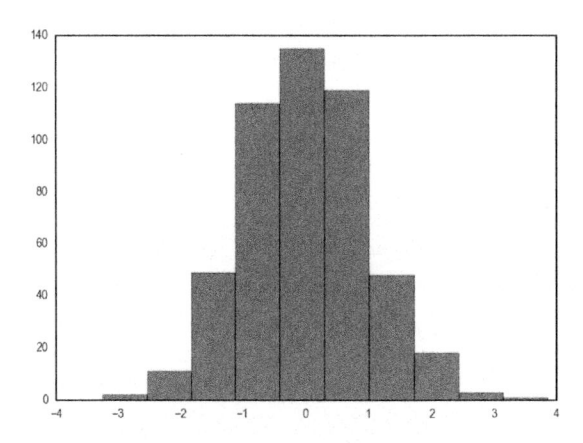

Figure 8.4: A histogram created by calling the matplotlib function directly.

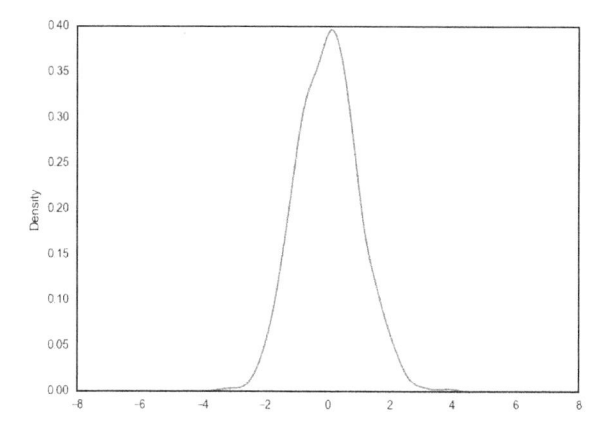

Figure 8.5: pandas can generate nice KDE charts if scipy.stats is installed

```
>>> fig.savefig('/tmp/ex4.png')
```

Because pandas plotting is built on top of the matplotlib library, we can use the underlying functionality to tweak out plots. Deep diving into matplotlib is beyond the scope of this book, but below you can see that we add 2 plots to the figure. On the first we plot a histogram and kernel density estimation. On the second, we plot a cumulative density plot:

```
>>> fig = plt.figure()
>>> ax = fig.add_subplot(211)
>>> data.plot(kind='kde', color='b', alpha=.6, ax=ax)   # requires sci
# normed=True is passed through to matplotlib
>>> data.hist(color='g', alpha=.6, ax=ax, normed=True)
>>> ax.set_title("KDE, Histogram & CDF")
>>> ax = fig.add_subplot(212)
>>> data.hist(ax=ax, normed=True, cumulative=True)
>>> fig.savefig('/tmp/ex5.png')
```

8.1 Other plot types

In addition, the series provides a few more options of out the box. The following table summarizes the different plots types. Not that these can be specified as kind parameters, or as attributes of the .plot attribute.

8. Series Plotting

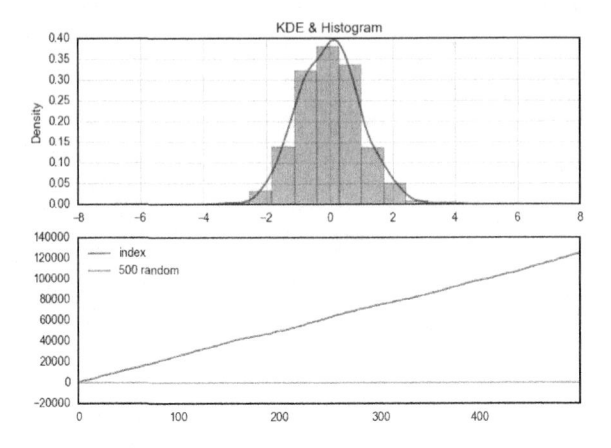

Figure 8.6: An illustration of using the matplotlib to create subplots

plot *Methods*	*Result*
plot.area	Creates an area plot for numeric columns
plot.bar	Creates a bar plot for numeric columns
plot.barh	Creates a horizonal bar plot for numeric columns
plot.box	Creates a box plot for numeric columns
plot.density	Creates a kernel density estimation plot for numeric columns (also plot.kde)
plot.hist	Creates a histogram for numeric columns
plot.line	Create a line plot. Plots index on x column, and numeric column values for y
plot.pie	Create a pie plot.

Another popular plotting option is to use the Seaborn[10] library. This library bills itself as a "Statistical data visualization" layer on top of matplotlib. It supports pandas natively, and has more plot types such as violin plots and swarm plots. It also offers the ability to *facet* charts (create subgrids based on features of the data). Given that both matplotlib and Seaborn offer a gallery on their website, feel free to browse the examples for inspiration.

---

[10]http://stanford.edu/~mwaskom/software/seaborn/

8.2 Summary

In this chapter we examined plotting a Series. The pandas library provides some hooks to the matplotlib library. These can be really convenient. When you need more power, you can drop into raw matplotlib commands. In the next chapter, we will wrap up our coverage of the Series, by looking at simple analysis.

Chapter 9

Another Series Example

I recently built an ergonomic keyboard[11]. To take full advantage of it, one might consider creating a custom keyboard layout by analyzing letter frequency. Since I tend to spend a lot of time programming, instead of just considering alphanumeric symbols, I should probably take into account programming symbols as well. Then I can be super efficient on my keyboard, eliminate RSI, and as an extra bonus, prevent others from using my computer! To work up to this, we will first consider an analysis of letter frequency.

Wikipedia has an entry on Letter Frequency[12], which contains a table and plot for relative frequencies of letters. Below is an attempt to recreate that table using pandas and the /usr/share/dict/american-english file found on many Linux distributions (or /usr/share/dict/words-english on Mac). This example will walk through getting the data into a Series object, tweaking it, and plotting the results.

9.1 Standard Python

To contrast between Python and pandas, we will process this data using both vanilla Python and then pandas. This should help you get a feel for the differences. We will start with the vanilla Python version.

Using Python's built-in string manipulation tools it is easy to count letter frequency. The dictionary file we will be analyzing contains data stored in plain text, one word per line:

---

[11]http://www.ergodox.org/

[12]http://en.wikipedia.org/wiki/Letter_frequency

9. Another Series Example

Figure 9.1: Both halves of my Ergodox keyboard in action.

9.1. Standard Python

```
$ head /usr/share/dict/american-english
A
A's
AA's
AB's
ABM's
AC's
ACTH's
AI's
AIDS's
AM's

$ tail /usr/share/dict/american-english
élan's
émigré
émigré's
émigrés
épée
épée's
épées
étude
étude's
```

First, we will load the data and store it in a variable. Note, that we are using Python 3 here, in Python 2 we would have to call .decode('utf=8') because the contains UTF-8 encoded accented characters:

```
>>> filename = '/usr/share/dict/american-english'
>>> data = open(filename).read()
```

Now, the newlines are removed and the results are flattened into a single string:

```
>>> data = ''.join(data.split())
```

With a big string containing the letters of all the words, the built-in class collections.Counter class makes easy work of counting letter frequency:

```
>>> from collections import Counter
>>> counts = Counter(data)
>>> counts
Counter({'s': 88663, 'e': 88237, 'i': 66643,
'a': 63151, 'r': 56645, 'n': 56626, 't': 52187,
'o': 48585, 'l': 40271, 'c': 30453, 'd': 27797,
'u"'": 26243, '': 25988, 'g': 21992, 'p': 21354,
'm': 20948, 'h': 18568, 'b': 14279, 'y': 12513,
'f': 10220, 'k': 7827, 'v': 7666, 'w': 7077,
'z': 3141, 'x': 2085, 'M': 1560, 'q': 1459,
'j': 1455, 'S': 1450, 'C': 1419, 'A': 1288,
'B': 1247, 'P': 920, 'L': 836, 'T': 819, 'H':
752, 'D': 734, 'G': 720, 'R': 702, 'E': 596,
'K': 582, 'N': 518, 'J': 493, 'F': 455, 'W':
453, 'O': 359, 'I': 343, 'V': 323, '\xe9': 144,
'Z': 140, 'Y': 139, '': 130, 'Q': 65, 'X':
```

9. Another Series Example

```
39, '\xe8': 28, '\xf6': 16, '\xfc': 12, '\xe1':
10, '\xf1': 8, '\xf3': 8, '\xe4': 7, '\xea': 6,
'\xe2': 6, '\xe7': 5, '\xe5': 3, '\xfb': 3,
'\xed': 2, '\xf4': 2, '\xc5': 1})
```

This is quick and dirty, though it has a few issues. Certainly the built-in Python tools could handle dealing with this data. But this book is discussing pandas, so let's look at the pandas version.

9.2 Enter pandas

First, we will load the words into a Series object. Because the shape of the data in the file is essentially a single column CSV file, the .from_csv method should handle it:

```
>>> words = pd.Series.from_csv(filename)
Traceback (most recent call last):
  ...
IndexError: single positional indexer is out-of-bounds
```

Whoops! The parsing logic is complaining because there is no index column. Let's try reading it again with index_col=None. This isn't well documented, but index_col=None tells pandas to create an index for us (it will just make an index of integers). We will also specify an encoding:

```
>>> words = pd.Series.from_csv(filename,
...     index_col=None, encoding='utf-8')
```

This should give us a series with a value for every word:

```
>>> words
0            A
1          A's
2         AA's
3         AB's
4        ABM's
5         AC's
6        ACTH's
7          AI's
8        AIDS's
9         AM's
10         AOL
11       AOL's
12      ASCII's
13       ASL's
14       ATM's
...
99156   éclair's
99157    éclairs
99158      éclat
99159    éclat's
99160       élan
99161     élan's
```

```
99162        émigré
99163        émigré's
99164        émigrés
99165        épée
99166        épée's
99167        épées
99168        étude
99169        étude's
99170        études
Length: 99171, dtype: object
```

At this point, it makes sense to think about what we want in the end. If we are sticking to the `Series` datatype, then a series that maps letters (as index values) to counts will probably allow basic analysis similar to Wikipedia. The question is how to get there?

One way is to create a new series, `counts`. This series will have letters in the index, and counts of those letters as the values. We can create it by iterating over the words using `apply` to add the count of every letter to `counts`. We will also lowercase the letters to normalize them:

```
>>> counts = pd.Series([], index=[])
>>> def update_counts(val):
...     global counts
...     for let in val:
...         let = let.lower()
...         count = counts.get(let, 0) + val.count(let)
...         counts = counts.set_value(let, count)

>>> _ = words.apply(update_counts)
```

Sort the counts based on the values:

```
>>> counts = counts.sort_values(ascending=False)
```

This will give us preliminary results:

```
>>> counts.head()
s    150525
e    148096
i    102818
a     91167
n     80992
dtype: int64
```

9.3 Tweaking data

The most common letter of the english language is normally "e" (which Wikipedia corroborates). How did "s" get up there? Looking at the original file shows that it has plural entries. Let's remove those and recount. One way to do that is to create a mask for all the words

9. Another Series Example

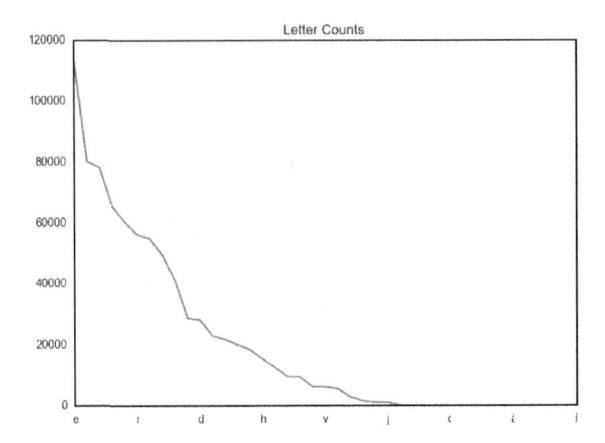

[Line plot titled "Letter Counts" with y-axis from 0 to 120000 and x-axis showing letters e, r, d, h, v, j, c, t, l]

Figure 9.2: Figure sowing the default plot of letter counts. Note that the default plot is a line plot.

containing ' in them. We will use the negation of that map to find the words without quotes:

```
>>> mask = ~(words.str.contains("'"))
>>> words = words[mask]
>>> counts = pd.Series([], index=[])
>>> _ = words.apply(update_counts)
>>> counts = counts.sort_values(ascending=False)
>>> counts.head()
e    113431
s     80170
i     78173
a     65492
n     60443
dtype: int64
```

That looks better. Let's plot it:

```
>>> fig = plt.figure()
>>> counts.plot(title="Letter Counts")
>>> fig.savefig('/tmp/letters1.png')
```

The default plot is a line plot. It is probably not the best visualization, and the ticks on the x axis are not very useful. Let's try a bar plot:

9.4. Custom symbol frequency

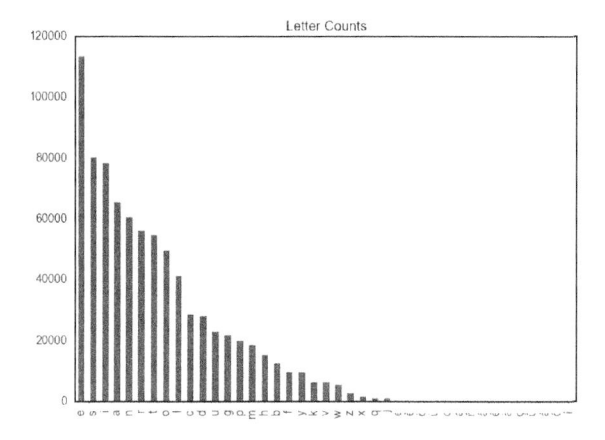

Figure 9.3: Figure showing a bar plot of letter counts.

```
>>> fig = plt.figure()
>>> counts.plot(kind='bar', title="Letter Counts")
>>> fig.savefig('/tmp/letters2.png')
```

That looks better. Wikipedia uses frequency rather than count. We can easily calculate frequency by applying the divide operation to the series with the sum as the denominator. Let's sort the index, so it is ordered alphabetically, and then plot it:

```
>>> fig = plt.figure()
>>> freq = counts/counts.sum()
>>> freq.sort_index().plot(kind='bar', title="Letter Frequency")
>>> fig.savefig('/tmp/letters3.png')
```

9.4 Custom symbol frequency

Here is perhaps an easier way to get character counts in a series. To determine frequency of symbols in a given file, we will treat the whole file as a list of characters (utf-8 encoded) including newlines. This turns out to be easier than loading the dictionary file.

First we will try out a get_freq function on a string buffer with dummy data to validate the functionality:

```
>>> def get_freq(fin):
...     ser = pd.Series(list(fin.read()))
...     ser = ser.value_counts()
```

81

9. Another Series Example

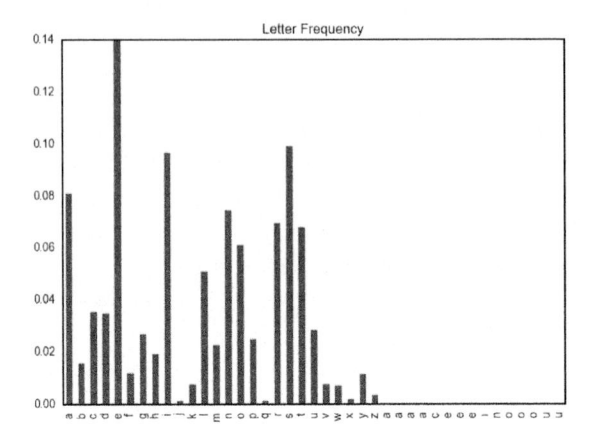

Figure 9.4: Figure showing a bar plot of letter frequencies.

```
...         return (ser * 100.) / ser.sum()
>>> fin = StringIO('abcabczzzzz\n\n')
>>> ser = get_freq(fin)
>>> ser
z      38.461538
\n     15.384615
b      15.384615
c      15.384615
a      15.384615
dtype: float64
```

I'll load it on the source of this book (which contains both the code and the text) and see what happens:

```
>>> ser = get_freq(open('template/pandas.rst'))
>>> ser
       23.553399
e       6.331422
t       4.672842
a       4.396412
s       3.753370
.       3.683772
i       3.521051
\n      3.472038
o       3.380875
n       3.206391
r       3.025045
l       2.351615
d       2.277116
=       1.938931
```

```
>         1.640935
...
ç         0.00196
Å         0.00196
è         0.00196
ñ         0.00196
ä         0.00196
?         0.00196
ê         0.00196
å         0.00196
ó         0.00196
^         0.00196
â         0.00196
á         0.00196
ô         0.00196
ö         0.00196
ü         0.00098
Length: 114, dtype: float64
```

A brief look at this indicates that the text of this book is abnormal relative to normal English. Also, were I to customize my keyboard based on this text, the non-alphabetic characters that I hit the most—space, period, return, equals, and greater than—should be pretty close to the home row. It seems that I need a larger corpus to sample from, and that my current keyboard layout is not optimal as the most popular characters do not have keys on the home row.

Again, we can visualize this quickly using the .plot method:

```
>>> fig = plt.figure()
>>> ser.plot(kind='bar', title="Custom Letter Frequency")
>>> fig.savefig('/tmp/letters4.png')
```

Note

I am currently typing with the Norman layout[13] on my ergonomic keyboard.

9.5 Summary

This chapter concludes our Series coverage. We examined loading data into a Series, processing it, and plotting it. We also saw how we could do similar processing with only the Python Standard Library. While that code is straightforward, once we start tweaking the data and plotting it, the pandas version becomes more concise, and will be faster.

---

[13]https://normanlayout.info/

9. Another Series Example

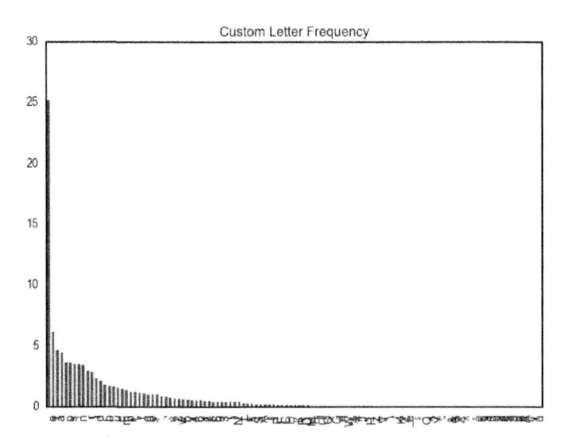

Figure 9.5: Figure showing letter frequency of the text of this book

Chapter 10

DataFrames

The two-dimensional counterpart to the one-dimensional Series is the DataFrame. To better understand this data structure, it helps to understand how it is constructed.

If you think of a data frame as row-oriented, the interface will feel wrong. Many tabular data structures are row-oriented. Perhaps this is due to spreadsheets and CSV files that are dealt with on a row by row basis. Perhaps it is due to the many OLTP[14] databases that are row oriented out of the box. A DataFrame, is often used for analytical purposes and is better understood when thought of as column oriented, where each column is a Series.

> **Note**
>
> In practice many highly optimized analytical databases (those used for OLAP cubes) are also column oriented. Laying out the data in a columnar manner can improve performance and require less resources. Columns of a single type can be compressed easily. Performing analysis on a column requires loading only that columns whereas a row oriented database would require loading the complete database to access an entire column.

Below is a simple attempt to create a tabular Python data structure that is column oriented. It has an 0-based integer index, but that

---

[14]*OLTP* (On-line Transaction Processing) is a characterization of databases that are meant for transactional data. Bank accounts are an example where data integrity is imperative, yet multiple users might need concurrent access. In contrast with *OLAP* (On-line Analytical Processing), which is optimized for complex querying and aggregation. Typically, reporting systems use these types of databases, which might store data in denormalized form in order to speed up access.

10. DataFrames

is not required, the index could be string based. Each column is similar to the Series-like structure developed previously:

```
>>> df = {
...     'index':[0,1,2],
...     'cols': [
...         { 'name':'growth',
...             'data':[.5, .7, 1.2] },
...         { 'name':'Name',
...             'data':['Paul', 'George', 'Ringo'] },
...         ]
... }
```

Rows are accessed via the index, and columns are accessible from the column name. Below are simple functions for accessing rows and columns:

```
>>> def get_row(df, idx):
...     results = []
...     value_idx = df['index'].index(idx)
...     for col in df['cols']:
...         results.append(col['data'][value_idx])
...     return results
>>> get_row(df, 1)
[0.7, 'George']

>>> def get_col(df, name):
...     for col in df['cols']:
...         if col['name'] == name:
...             return col['data']
>>> get_col(df, 'Name')
['Paul', 'George', 'Ringo']
```

10.1 DataFrames

Using the pandas `DataFrame` object, the previous data structure could be created like this:

```
>>> import pandas as pd
>>> df = pd.DataFrame({
...     'growth':[.5, .7, 1.2],
...     'Name':['Paul', 'George', 'Ringo'] })
>>> df
     Name   growth
0    Paul    0.5
1    George  0.7
2    Ringo   1.2
```

To access a row by location, index off of the `.iloc` attribute:

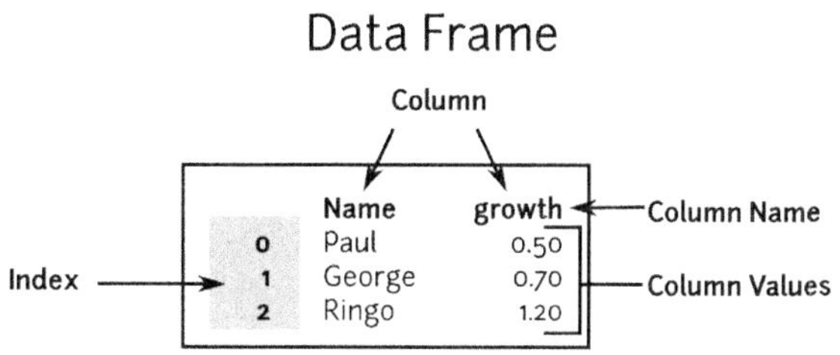

10.1. DataFrames

Data Frame

Figure 10.1: Figure showing column oriented nature of Data Frame. (Note that a column can be pulled off as a Series)

```
>>> df.iloc[2]
Name        Ringo
growth        1.2
Name: 2, dtype: object
```

Columns are accessible via indexing the column name off of the object:

```
>>> df['Name']
0      Paul
1    George
2     Ringo
Name: Name, dtype: object
```

Note the type of column is a pandas Series instance. Any operation that can be done to a series can be applied to a column:

```
>>> type(df['Name'])
<class 'pandas.core.series.Series'>
>>> df['Name'].str.lower()
0      paul
1    george
2     ringo
Name: Name, dtype: object
```

Note

The DataFrame overrides __getattr__ to allow access to columns as attributes. This tends to work ok, but will fail if the column name conflicts with an existing method or attribute, or has an unexpected character such as a space:

10. DATAFRAMES

```
>>> df.Name
0      Paul
1    George
2     Ringo
Name: Name, dtype: object
```

The above should provide hints as to why the `Series` was covered in such detail. When column operations are involved, a series method is often involved. In addition, the index behavior across both data structures is the same.

10.2 Construction

Data frames can be created from many types of input:

- columns (dicts of lists)
- rows (list of dicts)
- CSV file (`pd.read_csv`)
- from NumPy ndarray
- And more, SQL, HDF5, etc

The previous creation of `df` illustrated making a data frame from columns. Below is an example of creating a data frame from rows:

```
>>> pd.DataFrame([
...    {'growth':.5, 'Name':'Paul'},
...    {'growth':.7, 'Name':'George'},
...    {'growth':1.2, 'Name':'Ringo'}])
     Name  growth
0    Paul     0.5
1  George     0.7
2   Ringo     1.2
```

Similarly, here is an example of loading this data from a CSV file:

```
>>> csv_file = StringIO("""growth,Name
... .5,Paul
... .7,George
... 1.2,Ringo""")
>>> pd.read_csv(csv_file)
   growth    Name
0     0.5    Paul
1     0.7  George
2     1.2   Ringo
```

A data frame can be instantiated from a NumPy array as well. The column names will need to be specified:

88

10.3. Data Frame Axis

```
>>> pd.DataFrame(np.random.randn(10,3), columns=['a', 'b', 'c'])
          a         b         c
0  0.926178  1.909417 -1.398568
1  0.562969 -0.650643 -0.487125
2 -0.592394 -0.863991  0.048522
3 -0.830950  0.270457 -0.050238
4 -0.238948 -0.907564 -0.576771
5  0.755391  0.500917 -0.977555
6  0.099332  0.751387 -1.669405
7  0.543360 -0.662624  0.570599
8 -0.763259 -1.804882 -1.627542
9  0.048085  0.259723 -0.904317
```

10.3 Data Frame Axis

Unlike a series, which has one axis, there are two axes for a data frame. They are commonly referred to as axis 0 and 1, or the row/index axis and the columns axis respectively:

```
>>> df.axes
[RangeIndex(start=0, stop=3, step=1),
Index(['Name', 'growth'], dtype='object')]
```

As many operations take an axis parameter, it is important to remember that 0 is the index and 1 is the columns:

```
>>> df.axes[0]
RangeIndex(start=0, stop=3, step=1)

>>> df.axes[1]
Index(['Name', 'growth'], dtype='object')
```

Tip

In order to remember which axis is 0 and which is 1 it can be handy to think back to a Series. It also has *axis 0 along the index*:

```
>>> df = pd.DataFrame({'Score1': [None, None],
...                    'Score2': [85, 90]})
>>> df
  Score1  Score2
0   None      85
1   None      90
```

If we want to sum up each of the columns, the we sum along the index axis (axis=0), or along the row axis:

89

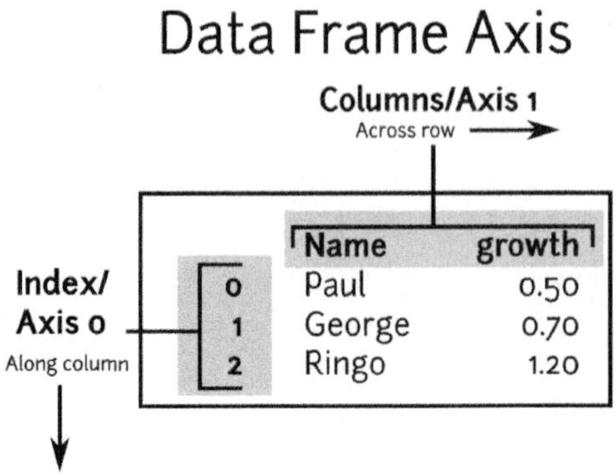

10. DATAFRAMES

Data Frame Axis

```
                    Columns/Axis 1
                    Across row ──►

                   ┌ Name      growth ┐
  Index/      0    │ Paul        0.50 │
  Axis 0      1    │ George      0.70 │
  Along column 2   └ Ringo       1.20 ┘
       │
       ▼
```

Figure 10.2: Figure showing relation between axis 0 and axis 1. Note that when an operation is applied along axis 0, it is applied down the column. Likewise, operations along axis 1 operate across the values in the row.

```
>>> df.apply(np.sum, axis=0)
Score1        NaN
Score2      175.0
dtype: float64
```

To sum along every row, we sum down the columns axis (axis=1):

```
>>> df.apply(np.sum, axis=1)
0    85
1    90
dtype: int64
```

10.4 Summary

In this section we were introduced to a Python data structure that is similar to how a pandas data frame is implemented. It illustrated the index and the columnar nature of the data frame. Then we looked at the main components of the data frame, and how columns are really just series objects. We saw various ways to construct data frames. Finally, we looked at the two axes of the data frame.

In future chapters we will dig in more and see the data frame in action.

Chapter 11

Data Frame Example

Before discussing data frames in detail, let's cover working with a small data set. Below is some data from a portion of trail data of the Wasatch 100 trail race[15]:

LOCATION	MILES	ELEVA-TION	CUMUL	% CUMUL GAIN
Big Mountain Pass Aid Station	39.07	7432	11579	43.8%
Mules Ear Meadow	40.75	7478	12008	45.4%
Bald Mountain	42.46	7869	12593	47.6%
Pence Point	43.99	7521	12813	48.4%
Alexander Ridge Aid Station	46.9	6160	13169	49.8%
Alexander Springs	47.97	5956	13319	50.3%
Rogers Trail junction	49.52	6698	13967	52.8%
Rogers Saddle	49.77	6790	14073	53.2%
Railroad Bed	50.15	6520		
Lambs Canyon Underpass Aid Station	52.48	6111	14329	54.2%
Lambs Trail	54.14	6628	14805	56.0%

We'll load this data into a data frame and use it data to show basic CRUD operations and plotting.

Reading in CSV files is straightforward in pandas. Here we paste the contents into a `StringIO` buffer to emulate a CSV file:

---

[15] Data existed at one point at http://www.wasatch100.com/index.php?option=com_content&view=article&id=132&Itemid=10

11. Data Frame Example

```
>>> data = StringIO('''LOCATION,MILES,ELEVATION,CUMUL,% CUMUL GAIN
... Big Mountain Pass Aid Station,39.07,7432,11579,43.8%
... Mules Ear Meadow,40.75,7478,12008,45.4%
... Bald Mountain,42.46,7869,12593,47.6%
... Pence Point,43.99,7521,12813,48.4%
... Alexander Ridge Aid Station,46.9,6160,13169,49.8%
... Alexander Springs,47.97,5956,13319,50.3%
... Rogers Trail junction,49.52,6698,13967,52.8%
... Rogers Saddle,49.77,6790,14073,53.2%
... Railroad Bed,50.15,6520,,
... Lambs Canyon Underpass Aid Station,52.48,6111,14329,54.2%''')

>>> df = pd.read_csv(data)
```

Now that the data is loaded, it can easily be examined:

```
>>> df
                              LOCATION  MILES  ELEVATION     CUMUL  % CUMUL
0           Big Mountain Pass Aid Station  39.07       7432   11579.0
43.8%
1                        Mules Ear Meadow  40.75       7478   12008.0
45.4%
2                           Bald Mountain  42.46       7869   12593.0
47.6%
3                             Pence Point  43.99       7521   12813.0
48.4%
4             Alexander Ridge Aid Station  46.90       6160   13169.0
49.8%
5                       Alexander Springs  47.97       5956   13319.0
50.3%
6                   Rogers Trail junction  49.52       6698   13967.0
52.8%
7                           Rogers Saddle  49.77       6790   14073.0
53.2%
8                            Railroad Bed  50.15       6520
NaN             NaN
9   Lambs Canyon Underpass Aid Station  52.48       6111   14329.0
54.2%
```

This book highlights a problem that a user may run across on a terminal. The pandas library tries to be smart about how it shows data on a terminal. In general it does a good job. Line wrapping can be annoying though if your terminal is not wide enough. One option is to invoke the .to_string method. To limit the width to a specific number of columns, the .to_string method accepts a line_width parameter:

```
>>> print(df.to_string(line_width=60))
                              LOCATION  MILES  ELEVATION  \
0           Big Mountain Pass Aid Station  39.07       7432
1                        Mules Ear Meadow  40.75       7478
2                           Bald Mountain  42.46       7869
3                             Pence Point  43.99       7521
4             Alexander Ridge Aid Station  46.90       6160
5                       Alexander Springs  47.97       5956
6                   Rogers Trail junction  49.52       6698
```

```
7                         Rogers Saddle  49.77      6790
8                           Railroad Bed  50.15      6520
9  Lambs Canyon Underpass Aid Station    52.48      6111

   CUMUL  % CUMUL GAIN
0  11579.0         43.8%
1  12008.0         45.4%
2  12593.0         47.6%
3  12813.0         48.4%
4  13169.0         49.8%
5  13319.0         50.3%
6  13967.0         52.8%
7  14073.0         53.2%
8      NaN           NaN
9  14329.0         54.2%
```

Another option for viewing data is to transpose it. This takes the columns and places them down the left side. Each row of the original data is now a column. In book form, neither of these options is nice with larger tables. Using a tool like Jupyter will allow you to see an HTML representation of the data:

```
>>> print(df.T.to_string(line_width=60))
                                     0  \
LOCATION      Big Mountain Pass Aid Station
MILES                            39.07
ELEVATION                         7432
CUMUL                            11579
% CUMUL GAIN                     43.8%

                              1              2  \
LOCATION      Mules Ear Meadow   Bald Mountain
MILES                    40.75           42.46
ELEVATION                 7478            7869
CUMUL                    12008           12593
% CUMUL GAIN             45.4%           47.6%

                         3                          4  \
LOCATION       Pence Point   Alexander Ridge Aid Station
MILES                43.99                          46.9
ELEVATION             7521                          6160
CUMUL                12813                         13169
% CUMUL GAIN         48.4%                         49.8%

                              5                      6  \
LOCATION      Alexander Springs  Rogers Trail junction
MILES                     47.97                  49.52
ELEVATION                  5956                   6698
CUMUL                     13319                  13967
% CUMUL GAIN              50.3%                  52.8%

                          7             8  \
LOCATION      Rogers Saddle  Railroad Bed
MILES                 49.77         50.15
ELEVATION              6790          6520
CUMUL                 14073           NaN
% CUMUL GAIN          53.2%           NaN
```

11. Data Frame Example

```
                                                 9
        LOCATION       Lambs Canyon Underpass Aid Station
        MILES                                        52.48
        ELEVATION                                     6111
        CUMUL                                        14329
        % CUMUL GAIN                                 54.2%
```

11.1 Looking at the data

In addition to just looking at the string representation of a data frame, the .describe method provides summary statistics of the numeric data. It returns the count of items, the average value, the standard deviation, and the range and quantile data for every column that is a float or and integer:

```
>>> df.describe()
            MILES     ELEVATION          CUMUL
count   10.000000     10.000000       9.000000
mean    46.306000   6853.500000   13094.444444
std      4.493574    681.391428     942.511686
min     39.070000   5956.000000   11579.000000
25%     42.842500   6250.000000   12593.000000
50%     47.435000   6744.000000   13169.000000
75%     49.707500   7466.500000   13967.000000
max     52.480000   7869.000000   14329.000000
```

Because every column can be treated as a series, the methods for analyzing the series can be used on the columns. The LOCATION column is string based, so we will use the .value_counts method to examine if there are repeats:

```
>>> df['LOCATION'].value_counts()
Railroad Bed                           1
Rogers Saddle                          1
Pence Point                            1
Alexander Springs                      1
Bald Mountain                          1
Lambs Canyon Underpass Aid Station     1
Mules Ear Meadow                       1
Big Mountain Pass Aid Station          1
Alexander Ridge Aid Station            1
Rogers Trail junction                  1
Name: LOCATION, dtype: int64
```

In this case, because the location names are unique, the .value_counts method does not provide much new information.

Another option for looking at the data is the .corr method. This method provides the *Pearson Correlation Coefficient* statistic for all the numeric columns in a table. The result is a number (between -1 and 1) that describes the linear relationship between the variables:

11.2. Plotting With Data Frames

```
>>> df.corr()
              MILES  ELEVATION     CUMUL
MILES      1.000000  -0.783780  0.986613
ELEVATION -0.783780   1.000000 -0.674333
CUMUL      0.986613  -0.674333  1.000000
```

This statistic shows that any column will have a perfect correlation (a value of 1) with itself, but also that cumulative elevation is pretty strongly correlated with distance (as both grow over the length of the course at a pretty constant rate, this makes intuitive sense). This is a section of the course where the starting point is at a higher elevation than the final elevation. As such, there is a negative correlation between the miles and elevation for this portion.

11.2 Plotting With Data Frames

Data frames also have built-in plotting ability. The default behavior is to use the index as the x values, and plot every numerical column (any string column is ignored):

```
>>> fig = plt.figure()
>>> df.plot()
>>> fig.savefig('/tmp/df-ex1.png')
```

The default saved plot is actually empty. (Note that if you are using Jupyter, this is not the case and a plot will appear if you used the %matplotlib inline directive). To save a plot of a data frame that has the image in it, the ax parameter needs to be passed a matplotlib Axis. Calling fig.subplot(111) will give us one:

```
>>> fig = plt.figure()
>>> ax = fig.add_subplot(111)
>>> df.plot(ax=ax)
>>> fig.savefig('/tmp/df-ex2.png')
```

These plots are not perfect, yet they start to show the power that pandas provides for visualizing data quickly.

The pandas library has some built-in support for the matplotlib library. Though there are a few quirks, we can easily produce charts and visualizations.

This plot has the problem that the scale of the miles plot is blown out due to the elevation numbers. pandas allows labelling the other y-axis (the one on the right side), but to do so requires two calls to .plot. For the first .plot call, pull out only the elevation columns using an index operation with a list of (numerical) columns to pull out. The second call will be made against the series with the mileage data and a secondary_y parameter set to True. It also requires an explicit call to plt.legend to place a legend for the mileage:

11. Data Frame Example

Figure 11.1: Default .plot of a data frame containing both numerical and string data. Note that when we try to save this as a png file it is empty if we forget the call to add a matplotlib axes to the figure (one way is to call fig.add_subplot(111)). Within Jupyter notebook, we will see a real plot, this is only an issue when using pandas to plot and then saving the plot.

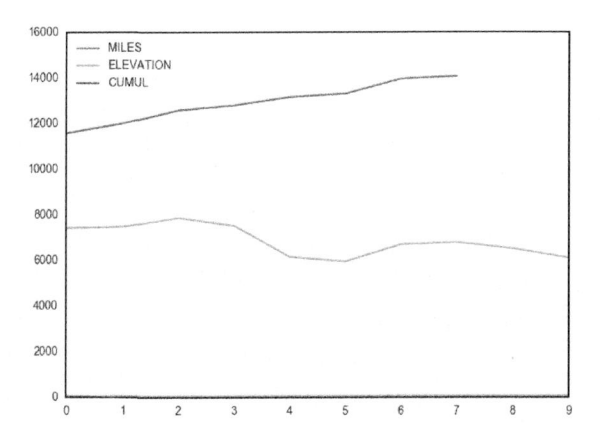

Figure 11.2: Default .plot of a data frame passing in the ax parameter so it saves correctly.

11.2. Plotting With Data Frames

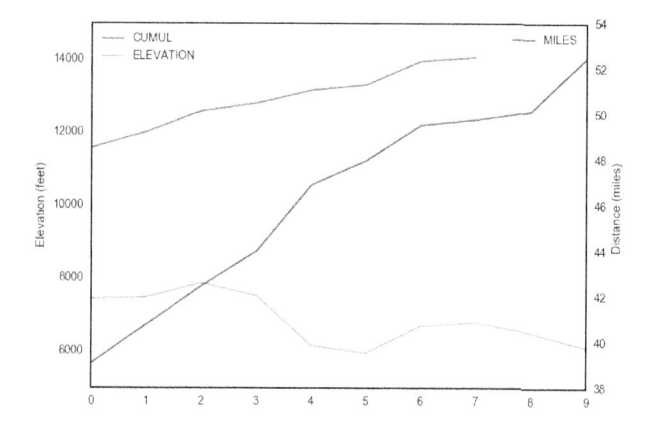

Figure 11.3: Plot using secondary_y parameter to use different scales on the left and right axis for elevation and distance.

```
>>> fig = plt.figure()
>>> ax = fig.add_subplot(111)
>>> df[['CUMUL', 'ELEVATION']].plot(ax=ax)
>>> df['MILES'].plot(secondary_y=True)
>>> plt.legend(loc='best')
>>> ax.set_ylabel('Elevation (feet)')
>>> ax.right_ax.set_ylabel('Distance (miles)')
>>> fig.savefig('/tmp/df-ex3.png')
```

Another way to convey information is to plot with labels along the x axis instead of using a numerical index (which does not mean much to viewers of the graph). By default, pandas plots the index along the x axis. To graph against the name of the station, we need to pass in an explicit value for x, the ELEVATION column. The labels will need to tilted a bit so that they do not overlap. This rotation is done with fig.autofmt_xdate(). The bounding box also needs to be expanded a bit so the labels do not get clipped off at the edges. The bbox_inches='tight' parameter to fig.savefig will help with this:

```
>>> fig = plt.figure()
>>> ax = fig.add_subplot(111)
>>> df.plot(x='LOCATION', y=['ELEVATION', 'CUMUL'], ax=ax)
>>> df.plot(x='LOCATION', y='MILES', secondary_y=True, ax=ax)
>>> ax.set_ylabel('Elevation (feet)')
>>> ax.right_ax.set_ylabel('Distance (miles)')
>>> fig.autofmt_xdate()
>>> fig.savefig('/tmp/df-ex4.png', bbox_inches='tight')
```

97

11. DATA FRAME EXAMPLE

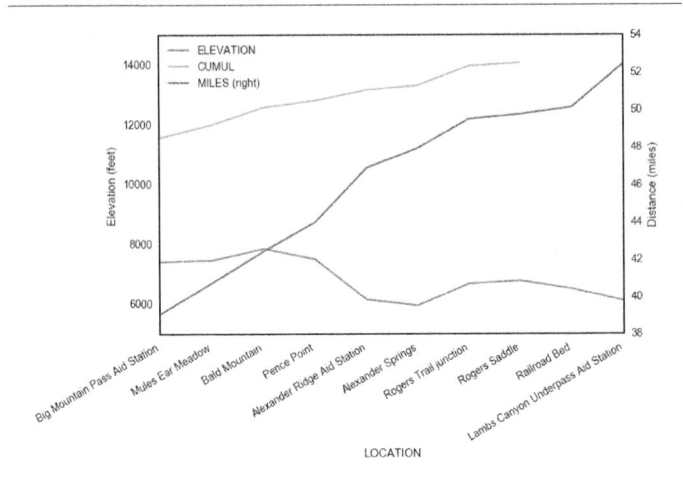

Figure 11.4: Plot using LOCATION as the x axis rather than the default (the index values).

Another option is to plot the elevation against the miles. pandas make it easy to experiment:

```
>>> fig = plt.figure()
>>> ax = fig.add_subplot(111)
>>> df.plot(x='MILES', y=['ELEVATION', 'CUMUL'], ax=ax)
>>> plt.legend(loc='best')
>>> ax.set_ylabel('Elevation (feet)')
>>> fig.savefig('/tmp/df-ex5.png')
```

11.3 Adding rows

The race data is a portion from the middle section of the race. If we wanted to combine the data with other portions of the trail, it requires using the .concat function or the .append method.

The .concat function combines two data frames. To add the next mile marker, we need to create a new data frame and use the function to join the two together:

```
>>> df2 = pd.DataFrame([('Lambs Trail',54.14,6628,14805,
...     '56.0%')], columns=['LOCATION','MILES','ELEVATION',
...     'CUMUL','% CUMUL GAIN'])
>>> print(pd.concat([df, df2]).to_string(line_width=60))
                      LOCATION    MILES   ELEVATION  \
0      Big Mountain Pass Aid Station   39.07       7432
1                   Mules Ear Meadow   40.75       7478
```

11.3. Adding rows

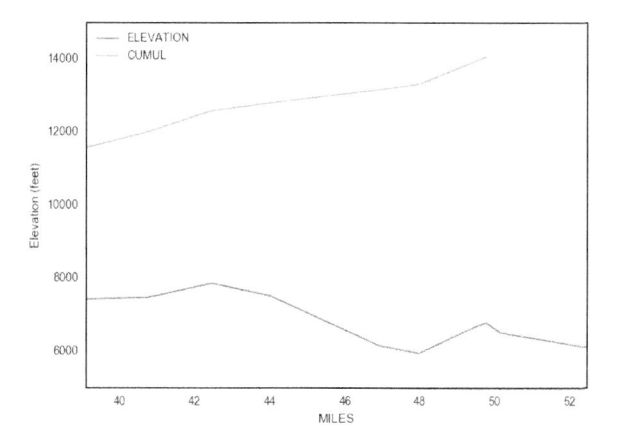

Figure 11.5: Plot using MILES as the x axis rather than the default (the index values).

```
2                    Bald Mountain  42.46  7869
3                      Pence Point  43.99  7521
4       Alexander Ridge Aid Station  46.90  6160
5               Alexander Springs   47.97  5956
6             Rogers Trail junction  49.52  6698
7                    Rogers Saddle  49.77  6790
8                     Railroad Bed  50.15  6520
9   Lambs Canyon Underpass Aid Station  52.48  6111
0                      Lambs Trail  54.14  6628

      CUMUL  % CUMUL GAIN
0   11579.0         43.8%
1   12008.0         45.4%
2   12593.0         47.6%
3   12813.0         48.4%
4   13169.0         49.8%
5   13319.0         50.3%
6   13967.0         52.8%
7   14073.0         53.2%
8      NaN           NaN
9   14329.0         54.2%
0   14805.0         56.0%
```

There are a couple of things to note from the result of this operation:

- The original data frames were not modified. This is usually (but not always) the case with pandas data structures.
- The index of the last entry is 0. Ideally it would be 10.

11. Data Frame Example

To resolve the last issue, pass the ignore_index=True parameter to concat. To solve the first issue, simply overwrite df with the new data frame:

```
>>> df = pd.concat([df, df2], ignore_index=True)
>>> df.index
Int64Index([0, 1, 2, 3, 4, 5, 6, 7, 8, 9, 10], dtype='int64')
```

11.4 Adding columns

To add a column, simply assign a series to a new column name:

```
>>> df['bogus'] = pd.Series(range(11))
```

Below, we add a column named STATION, based on whether the location has an aid station. It will compute the new boolean value for the column based on the occurrence of 'Station' in the LOCATION column:

```
>>> def aid_station(val):
...     return 'Station' in val

>>> df['STATION'] = df['LOCATION'].apply(aid_station)
>>> print(df.to_string(line_width=60))
                         LOCATION  MILES  ELEVATION  \
0     Big Mountain Pass Aid Station  39.07       7432
1                 Mules Ear Meadow  40.75       7478
2                     Bald Mountain  42.46       7869
3                       Pence Point  43.99       7521
4      Alexander Ridge Aid Station  46.90       6160
5                 Alexander Springs  47.97       5956
6             Rogers Trail junction  49.52       6698
7                    Rogers Saddle  49.77       6790
8                     Railroad Bed  50.15       6520
9   Lambs Canyon Underpass Aid Station  52.48   6111
10                     Lambs Trail  54.14       6628

    CUMUL  % CUMUL GAIN  bogus STATION
0   11579.0        43.8%      0    True
1   12008.0        45.4%      1   False
2   12593.0        47.6%      2   False
3   12813.0        48.4%      3   False
4   13169.0        49.8%      4    True
5   13319.0        50.3%      5   False
6   13967.0        52.8%      6   False
7   14073.0        53.2%      7   False
8       NaN          NaN      8   False
9   14329.0        54.2%      9    True
10  14805.0        56.0%     10   False
```

11.5 Deleting Rows

The pandas data frame has a `.drop` method that takes a sequence of index values. It returns a new data frame without those index entries. To remove the items found in index 5 and 9 use the following:

```
>>> df.drop([5, 9])
                      LOCATION   MILES   ELEVATION    CUMUL  % CUMUL GA
0    Big Mountain Pass Aid Station   39.07       7432    11579
43.8%       True
1                 Mules Ear Meadow   40.75       7478    12008
45.4%      False
2                    Bald Mountain   42.46       7869    12593
47.6%      False
3                      Pence Point   43.99       7521    12813
48.4%      False
4     Alexander Ridge Aid Station   46.90       6160    13169
49.8%       True
6             Rogers Trail junction   49.52       6698    13967
52.8%      False
7                    Rogers Saddle   49.77       6790    14073
53.2%      False
8                     Railroad Bed   50.15       6520      NaN
NaN        False
10                     Lambs Trail   54.14       6628    14805
56.0%      False
```

Note

The `.drop` method does not work in place. It returns a new data frame.

This method accepts index labels, which can be pulled out by slicing the `.index` attribute as well. This is useful when using text indexes or to delete large slices of rows. The previous example can be written as:

```
>>> df.drop(df.index[5:10:4])
                      LOCATION   MILES   ELEVATION    CUMUL  % CUMUL GA
0    Big Mountain Pass Aid Station   39.07       7432    11579
43.8%       True
1                 Mules Ear Meadow   40.75       7478    12008
45.4%      False
2                    Bald Mountain   42.46       7869    12593
47.6%      False
3                      Pence Point   43.99       7521    12813
48.4%      False
4     Alexander Ridge Aid Station   46.90       6160    13169
49.8%       True
6             Rogers Trail junction   49.52       6698    13967
52.8%      False
7                    Rogers Saddle   49.77       6790    14073
53.2%      False
8                     Railroad Bed   50.15       6520      NaN
NaN        False
```

11. Data Frame Example

```
10                      Lambs Trail   54.14      6628   14805
56.0%     False
```

11.6 Deleting Columns

To delete columns, use the .pop method, the .drop method with axis=1, or the del statement. Since the bogus column provides no additional value over the index, we will drop it:

```
>>> bogus = df.pop('bogus')
```

The bogus object is now a series holding the column removed from the data frame:

```
>>> bogus
0      0
1      1
2      2
3      3
4      4
5      5
6      6
7      7
8      8
9      9
10    10
Name: bogus, dtype: int64
```

Examining the columns shows that bogus no longer exists:

```
>>> df.columns
Index(['LOCATION', 'MILES', 'ELEVATION', 'CUMUL',
'% CUMUL GAIN', 'STATION'], dtype='object')
```

Because data frames emulate some of the dictionary interface, the del statement can also be used to remove columns. First, we will add the column back before deleting it again:

```
>>> df['bogus'] = bogus
>>> del df['bogus']

>>> df.columns
Index(['LOCATION', 'MILES', 'ELEVATION', 'CUMUL',
'% CUMUL GAIN', 'STATION'], dtype='object')
```

Note

These operations operate on the data frame *in place*.

The .drop method accepts an axis parameter and does not work in place—it returns a new data frame:

```
>>> df.drop(['ELEVATION', 'CUMUL', '% CUMUL GAIN', 'STATION'],
...     axis=1)
                          LOCATION  MILES
0        Big Mountain Pass Aid Station  39.07
1                    Mules Ear Meadow  40.75
2                       Bald Mountain  42.46
3                         Pence Point  43.99
4          Alexander Ridge Aid Station  46.90
5                   Alexander Springs  47.97
6                Rogers Trail junction  49.52
7                       Rogers Saddle  49.77
8                        Railroad Bed  50.15
9       Lambs Canyon Underpass Aid Station  52.48
10                        Lambs Trail  54.14
```

Note

It will be more consistent to use .drop with axis=1 than del or .pop. You will have to get used to the meaning of axis=1, which you can interpret as "apply this to the columns".

Working with this data should give you a feeling for the kinds of operations that are possible on DataFrame objects. This section has only covered a small portion of them.

11.7 Summary

In this chapter, we saw a quick overview of the data frame. We saw how to load data from a CSV file. We also looked at CRUD operations and plotting data.

In the next chapter we will examine the various members of the DataFrame object.

Chapter 12

Data Frame Methods

Part of the power of pandas is due to the rich methods that are built-in to the Series and DataFrame objects. This chapter will look into many of the attributes of the DataFrame.

The data for this section is sample retail sales data:

```
>>> data = StringIO('''UPC,Units,Sales,Date
... 1234,5,20.2,1-1-2014
... 1234,2,8.,1-2-2014
... 1234,3,13.,1-3-2014
... 789,1,2.,1-1-2014
... 789,2,3.8,1-2-2014
... 789,,,1-3-2014
... 789,1,1.8,1-5-2014''')

>>> sales = pd.read_csv(data)
>>> sales
    UPC  Units  Sales      Date
0  1234    5.0   20.2  1-1-2014
1  1234    2.0    8.0  1-2-2014
2  1234    3.0   13.0  1-3-2014
3   789    1.0    2.0  1-1-2014
4   789    2.0    3.8  1-2-2014
5   789    NaN    NaN  1-3-2014
6   789    1.0    1.8  1-5-2014
```

12.1 Data Frame Attributes

Let's dig in a little more. We can examine the axes of a data frame by looking at the .axes attribute:

```
>>> sales.axes
[RangeIndex(start=0, stop=7, step=1),
 Index(['UPC', 'Units', 'Sales', 'Date'], dtype='object')]
```

12. Data Frame Methods

The .axes is a list that contains the index and columns:

```
>>> sales.index
RangeIndex(start=0, stop=7, step=1)

>>> sales.columns
Index(['UPC', 'Units', 'Sales', 'Date'],
dtype='object')
```

The number of row and columns is also available via the .shape attribute:

```
>>> sales.shape
(7, 4)
```

For basic information about the object, use the .info method. Notice that the dtype for UPC is int64. Though UPC appears number-like here, it is possible to have dashes or other non-numeric values. It might be preferable to have it stored as a string. Also, the dtype for Date is object, it would be nice if it was a date instead. This may prove problematic when doing actual analysis. In later sections we will show how to change these types using the .astype method and the to_datetime function.

The .info method summarizes the types and columns of a data frame. It also provides insight into how much memory is being consumed. When you have larger data sets, this information is useful to see where memory is going. Converting string types to numeric or date types can go far to help lower the memory usage:

```
>>> sales.info()
<class 'pandas.core.frame.DataFrame'>
Int64Index: 7 entries, 0 to 6
Data columns (total 4 columns):
UPC      7 non-null int64
Units    6 non-null float64
Sales    6 non-null float64
Date     7 non-null object
dtypes: float64(2), int64(1), object(1)
memory usage: 280.0+ bytes
```

12.2 Iteration

Data frames include a variety of methods to iterate over the values. By default, iteration occurs over the column names:

```
>>> for column in sales:
...     print(column)
UPC
Units
Sales
Date
```

12.2. Iteration

The .keys method is a more explicit synonym for the default iteration behavior:

```
>>> for column in sales.keys():
...     print(column)
UPC
Units
Sales
Date
```

Note

Unlike the Series object which tests for membership against the index, the DataFrame tests for membership against the columns. The iteration behavior (__iter__) and membership behavior (__contains__) is the same for the DataFrame:

```
>>> 'Units' in sales
True

>>> 0 in sales
False
```

The .iteritems method returns pairs of column names and the individual column (as a Series):

```
>>> for col, ser in sales.iteritems():
...     print(col, ser)
UPC 0    1234
1    1234
2    1234
3     789
4     789
5     789
6     789
Name: UPC, dtype: int64
Units 0    5.0
1    2.0
2    3.0
3    1.0
4    2.0
5    NaN
6    1.0
Name: Units, dtype: float64
Sales 0    20.2
1     8.0
2    13.0
3     2.0
4     3.8
5     NaN
6     1.8
Name: Sales, dtype: float64
Date 0    1-1-2014
1    1-2-2014
```

107

12. Data Frame Methods

```
2      1-3-2014
3      1-1-2014
4      1-2-2014
5      1-3-2014
6      1-5-2014
Name: Date, dtype: object
```

The .iterrows method returns a tuple for every row. The tuple has two items. The first is the index value. The second is the row converted into a Series object. This might be a little tricky in practice because a row's values might not be homogenous, whereas that is usually the case in a column of data. Notice that the dtype for the row series is object because the row has strings and numeric values in it:

```
>>> for row in sales.iterrows():
...     print(row)
...     break   # limit data
(0, UPC         1234
Units             5
Sales          20.2
Date       1-1-2014
Name: 0, dtype: object)
```

The .itertuples method returns a namedtuple containing the index and row values:

```
>>> for row in sales.itertuples():
...     print(row)
...     break   # limit data
Pandas(Index=0, UPC=1234, Units=5.0, Sales=20.199999999999999, Date='1-1-2014')
```

Note

If you aren't familiar with NamedTuples in Python, check them out from the collections module. They give you all the benefits of a tuple: immutable, low memory requirements, and index access. In addition, the namedtuple allows you to access values by attribute:

```
>>> import collections
>>> Sales = collections.namedtuple('Sales',
...          'upc,units,sales')

>>> s = Sales(1234, 5., 20.2)
>>> s[0]   # index access
1234
>>> s.upc  # attribute access
1234
```

This helps make your code more readable, as 0 is a *magic number* in the above code. It is not clear to readers of the code what 0 is. But .upc is very explicit and makes for readable code.

We can ask a data frame how long it is with the len function. This is not the number of columns (even though iteration is over the columns), but the number of rows:

```
>>> len(sales)   # len of rows/index
7
```

Note

Operations performed during iteration are not *vectorized* in pandas and have overhead. If you find yourself performing operations in an iteration loop, there might be a vectorized way to do the same thing.

For example, you would not want to iterate over the row data to sum the column values. The .sum method is optimized to perform this operation.

12.3 Arithmetic

Data frames support *broadcasting* of arithmetic operations. If we add a number to a data frame, it is possible to increment every cell by that amount. But there is a caveat, to increment every numeric value by ten, simply adding ten to the data frame will fail:

```
>>> sales + 10
Traceback (most recent call last):
  ...
TypeError: Could not operate 10 with block values
Can't convert 'int' object to str implicitly
```

We need to only broadcast this operation to the numeric columns. Since the units and sales columns are both numeric, we can slice them out and broadcast on them:

```
>>> sales[['Sales', 'Units']] + 10
   Sales  Units
0   30.2   15.0
1   18.0   12.0
2   23.0   13.0
3   12.0   11.0
4   13.8   12.0
5    NaN    NaN
6   11.8   11.0
```

12. Data Frame Methods

In practice, unless the data columns are homogenous, such operations will be performed on a subset of the columns. To adjust only the units column, simply broadcast to that column:

```
>>> sales.Units + 2
0    7.0
1    4.0
2    5.0
3    3.0
4    4.0
5    NaN
6    3.0
Name: Units, dtype: float64
```

12.4 Matrix Operations

The data frame can be treated as a matrix. There is support for transposing a matrix:

```
>>> sales.transpose()    # sales.T is a shortcut
             0          1          2          3          4          5          6
UPC       1234       1234       1234        789        789        789        789
Units        5          2          3          1          2        NaN          1
Sales     20.2          8         13          2        3.8        NaN        1.8
Date  1-1-2014   1-2-2014   1-3-2014   1-1-2014   1-2-2014   1-3-2014   1-5-2014
```

Tip

The .T property of a data frame is a nice wrapper to the .transpose method. It comes in handy when examining a data frame in an iPython Notebook. It turns out that viewing the column headers along the left-hand side often makes the data more compact and easier to read.

The dot product can be called on a data frame if the contents are numeric:

```
>>> sales.dot(sales.T)
Traceback (most recent call last):
  ...
TypeError: can't multiply sequence by non-int of type 'str'
```

12.5 Serialization

Data frames can serialize to many forms. The most important functionality is probably converting to and from a CSV file, as this format is the lingua franca of data. We already saw that the pd.read_csv function will create a DataFrame. Writing to CSV is easy, we simply use the .to_csv method:

```
>>> fout = StringIO()
>>> sales.to_csv(fout, index_label='index')

>>> print(fout.getvalue())
index,UPC,Units,Sales,Date
0,1234,5.0,20.2,1-1-2014
1,1234,2.0,8.0,1-2-2014
2,1234,3.0,13.0,1-3-2014
3,789,1.0,2.0,1-1-2014
4,789,2.0,3.8,1-2-2014
5,789,,,1-3-2014
6,789,1.0,1.8,1-5-2014
```

The .to_dict method gives a mapping of column name to a mapping of index to value. If you needed to store the data in a JSON compliant format, this is one possibility:

```
>>> sales.to_dict()
{'Units': {0: 5.0, 1: 2.0, 2: 3.0, 3: 1.0, 4: 2.0,
    5: nan, 6: 1.0},
 'Date': {0: '1-1-2014', 1: '1-2-2014', 2: '1-3-2014',
    3: '1-1-2014', 4: '1-2-2014', 5: '1-3-2014',
    6: '1-5-2014'},
 'UPC': {0: 1234, 1: 1234, 2: 1234, 3: 789, 4: 789,
    5: 789, 6: 789},
 'Sales': {0: 20.2, 1: 8.0, 2: 13.0, 3: 2.0, 4: 3.8,
    5: nan, 6: 1.8}}
```

An optional parameter orient can create a mapping of column name to a list of values:

```
>>> sales.to_dict(orient='list')
{'Units': [5.0, 2.0, 3.0, 1.0, 2.0, nan, 1.0],
 'Date': ['1-1-2014', '1-2-2014', '1-3-2014',
 '1-1-2014', '1-2-2014', '1-3-2014', '1-5-2014'],
 'UPC': [1234, 1234, 1234, 789, 789, 789, 789],
 'Sales': [20.2, 8.0, 13.0, 2.0, 3.8, nan, 1.8]}
```

Data frames can also be created from the serialized dict if needed:

```
>>> pd.DataFrame.from_dict(sales.to_dict())
       Date  Sales   UPC  Units
0  1-1-2014   20.2  1234    5.0
1  1-2-2014    8.0  1234    2.0
2  1-3-2014   13.0  1234    3.0
3  1-1-2014    2.0   789    1.0
4  1-2-2014    3.8   789    2.0
```

12. Data Frame Methods

```
5  1-3-2014    NaN    789    NaN
6  1-5-2014    1.8    789    1.0
```

In addition, data frames can read and write Excel files. Use the `.to_excel` method to dump the data out:

```
>>> writer = pd.ExcelWriter('/tmp/output.xlsx')
>>> sales.to_excel(writer, 'sheet1')
>>> writer.save()
```

We can also read Excel data:

```
>>> pd.read_excel('/tmp/output.xlsx')
    UPC    Units   Sales    Date
0   1234    5.0    20.2     1-1-2014
1   1234    2.0     8.0     1-2-2014
2   1234    3.0    13.0     1-3-2014
3    789    1.0     2.0     1-1-2014
4    789    2.0     3.8     1-2-2014
5    789    NaN     NaN     1-3-2014
6    789    1.0     1.8     1-5-2014
```

Note

You might need to install the openpypxl module to support reading and writing xlsx to Excel. This is easy with `pip`:

```
$ pip install openpyxl
```

If you are dealing with xls files, you will need xlrd and xlwt. Again, pip makes this easy:

```
$ pip install xlrd xlwt
```

Note

The read_excel function has many options to help it divine how to parse spreadsheets that aren't simply CSV files that are loaded into Excel. You might need to play around with them. Often, it is easier (but perhaps not quite as satisfying) to open a spreadsheet and simply export a new sheet with only the data you need.

Data frames can also be converted to NumPy matrices for use in applications that support them:

```
>>> sales.as_matrix()   # NumPy representation
array([[1234, 5.0, 20.2, '1-1-2014'],
       [1234, 2.0, 8.0, '1-2-2014'],
       [1234, 3.0, 13.0, '1-3-2014'],
       [789, 1.0, 2.0, '1-1-2014'],
```

12.6 Index Operations

```
               [789, 2.0, 3.8, '1-2-2014'],
               [789, nan, nan, '1-3-2014'],
               [789, 1.0, 1.8, '1-5-2014']], dtype=object)
```

12.6 Index Operations

A data frame has various index operations. The first that we will explore—`.reindex`—conforms the data to a new index and/or columns. To pull out just the items at index 0 and 4, do the following:

```
>>> sales.reindex([0, 4])
    UPC  Units  Sales      Date
0  1234    5.0   20.2  1-1-2014
4   789    2.0    3.8  1-2-2014
```

This method also supports column selection:

```
>>> sales.reindex(columns=['Date', 'Sales'])
       Date  Sales
0  1-1-2014   20.2
1  1-2-2014    8.0
2  1-3-2014   13.0
3  1-1-2014    2.0
4  1-2-2014    3.8
5  1-3-2014    NaN
6  1-5-2014    1.8
```

Column and index selection may be combined to further refine selection. In addition, new entries for both index values and column names can be included. They will default to the `fill_value` optional parameter (which is NaN unless specified):

```
>>> sales.reindex(index=[2, 6, 8],
...       columns=['Sales', 'UPC', 'missing'])
   Sales     UPC  missing
2   13.0  1234.0      NaN
6    1.8   789.0      NaN
8    NaN     NaN      NaN
```

One common operation is to use another column as the index. The `.set_index` method does this for us:

```
>>> by_date = sales.set_index('Date')
>>> by_date
           UPC  Units  Sales
Date
1-1-2014  1234    5.0   20.2
1-2-2014  1234    2.0    8.0
1-3-2014  1234    3.0   13.0
1-1-2014   789    1.0    2.0
1-2-2014   789    2.0    3.8
1-3-2014   789    NaN    NaN
1-5-2014   789    1.0    1.8
```

12. Data Frame Methods

Note

Be careful, if you think of the index as analogous to a primary key in database parlance. Because the index can contain duplicate entries, this description is not quite accurate. Use the verify_integrity parameter to ensure uniqueness:

```
>>> sales.set_index('Date', verify_integrity=True)
Traceback (most recent call last):
...
ValueError: Index has duplicate keys: ['1-1-2014',
'1-2-2014', '1-3-2014']
```

To add an incrementing integer index to a data frame, use .reset_index:

```
>>> by_date.reset_index()
      Date  UPC  Units  Sales
0  1-1-2014  1234    5.0   20.2
1  1-2-2014  1234    2.0    8.0
2  1-3-2014  1234    3.0   13.0
3  1-1-2014   789    1.0    2.0
4  1-2-2014   789    2.0    3.8
5  1-3-2014   789    NaN    NaN
6  1-5-2014   789    1.0    1.8
```

12.7 Getting and Setting Values

There are two methods to pull out a single "cell" in the data frame. One—.iat—uses the position of the index and column (0-based):

```
>>> sales.iat[4, 2]
3.7999999999999998
```

The other option—.get_value—uses an index name and a column name:

```
>>> by_date.get_value('1-5-2014', 'UPC')
789
```

Again, if a duplicate valued index is selected, the result will not be a scalar, but will be an array (or possibly a data frame):

```
>>> by_date.get_value('1-2-2014', 'UPC')
array([1234,  789])
```

The .get_value method has an analog—.set_value—to assign a scalar to an index and column value. To assign sales of 789 to index 6 (yes that happens to also be a UPC value), do the following:

12.7. Getting and Setting Values

```
>>> sales.set_value(6, 'Sales', 789)
    UPC  Units  Sales      Date
0  1234    5.0   20.2  1-1-2014
1  1234    2.0    8.0  1-2-2014
2  1234    3.0   13.0  1-3-2014
3   789    1.0    2.0  1-1-2014
4   789    2.0    3.8  1-2-2014
5   789    NaN    NaN  1-3-2014
6   789    1.0  789.0  1-5-2014
```

There is no `.iset_value` method.

To insert a column at a specified location use the `.insert` method. Note that this method operates in-place and does not have a return value. The first parameter for the method is the zero-based location of the new column. The next parameter is the new column name and the third parameter is the new value. Below we insert a category column after UPC (at position 1):

```
>>> sales.insert(1, 'Category', 'Food')

# no return value!

>>> sales
    UPC Category  Units  Sales      Date
0  1234     Food    5.0   20.2  1-1-2014
1  1234     Food    2.0    8.0  1-2-2014
2  1234     Food    3.0   13.0  1-3-2014
3   789     Food    1.0    2.0  1-1-2014
4   789     Food    2.0    3.8  1-2-2014
5   789     Food    NaN    NaN  1-3-2014
6   789     Food    1.0  789.0  1-5-2014
```

The value does not have to be a scalar, it could be a sequence or a `Series` object, in which case it should have the same length as the data frame.

Note

Column insertion is also available through index assignment on the data frame. When new columns are added this way, they are always appended to the end (the right-most column). To change the order of the columns calling `.reindex` or indexing with the list of desired columns would be necessary.

The `.replace` method is a powerful way to update many values of a data frame across columns. To replace all 789's with 790 do the following:

```
>>> sales.replace(789, 790)
    UPC Category  Units  Sales      Date
0  1234     Food    5.0   20.2  1-1-2014
1  1234     Food    2.0    8.0  1-2-2014
2  1234     Food    3.0   13.0  1-3-2014
3   790     Food    1.0    2.0  1-1-2014
```

12. Data Frame Methods

```
4  790  Food  2.0   3.8   1-2-2014
5  790  Food  NaN   NaN   1-3-2014
6  790  Food  1.0  790.0  1-5-2014
```

Because the sales column for index 6 also has a value of 789, this will be replaced as well. To fix this, instead of passing in a scalar for the to_replace parameter, use a dictionary mapping column name to a dictionary of value to new value. If the new sales value of 789.0 was also erroneous, it could be updated in the same call:

```
>>> sales.replace({'UPC': {789: 790},
...               'Sales': {789: 1.4}})
   UPC  Category  Units  Sales      Date
0  1234    Food     5.0   20.2  1-1-2014
1  1234    Food     2.0    8.0  1-2-2014
2  1234    Food     3.0   13.0  1-3-2014
3   790    Food     1.0    2.0  1-1-2014
4   790    Food     2.0    3.8  1-2-2014
5   790    Food     NaN    NaN  1-3-2014
6   790    Food     1.0    1.4  1-5-2014
```

The .replace method will also accept regular expressions (they can also be included in nested dictionaries) if the regex parameter is set to True:

```
>>> sales.replace('(F.*d)', r'\1_stuff', regex=True)
   UPC    Category  Units  Sales      Date
0  1234  Food_stuff   5.0   20.2  1-1-2014
1  1234  Food_stuff   2.0    8.0  1-2-2014
2  1234  Food_stuff   3.0   13.0  1-3-2014
3   789  Food_stuff   1.0    2.0  1-1-2014
4   789  Food_stuff   2.0    3.8  1-2-2014
5   789  Food_stuff   NaN    NaN  1-3-2014
6   789  Food_stuff   1.0  789.0  1-5-2014
```

12.8 Deleting Columns

There are at least four ways to remove a column:

- The .pop method
- The .drop method with axis=1
- The .reindex method
- Indexing with a list of new columns

The .pop method takes the name of a column and removes it from the data frame. It operates in-place. Rather than returning a data frame, it returns the removed column. Below, the column subcat will be added and then subsequently removed:

12.8. Deleting Columns

```
>>> sales['subcat'] = 'Dairy'
>>> sales
    UPC Category  Units  Sales       Date subcat
0  1234     Food    5.0   20.2   1-1-2014  Dairy
1  1234     Food    2.0    8.0   1-2-2014  Dairy
2  1234     Food    3.0   13.0   1-3-2014  Dairy
3   789     Food    1.0    2.0   1-1-2014  Dairy
4   789     Food    2.0    3.8   1-2-2014  Dairy
5   789     Food    NaN    NaN   1-3-2014  Dairy
6   789     Food    1.0  789.0   1-5-2014  Dairy
>>> sales.pop('subcat')
0    Dairy
1    Dairy
2    Dairy
3    Dairy
4    Dairy
5    Dairy
6    Dairy
Name: subcat, dtype: object
>>> sales
    UPC Category  Units  Sales       Date
0  1234     Food    5.0   20.2   1-1-2014
1  1234     Food    2.0    8.0   1-2-2014
2  1234     Food    3.0   13.0   1-3-2014
3   789     Food    1.0    2.0   1-1-2014
4   789     Food    2.0    3.8   1-2-2014
5   789     Food    NaN    NaN   1-3-2014
6   789     Food    1.0  789.0   1-5-2014
```

To drop a column with the .drop method, simply pass it in (or a list of column names) along with setting the axis parameter to 1:

```
>>> sales.drop(['Category', 'Units'], axis=1)
    UPC  Sales       Date
0  1234   20.2   1-1-2014
1  1234    8.0   1-2-2014
2  1234   13.0   1-3-2014
3   789    2.0   1-1-2014
4   789    3.8   1-2-2014
5   789    NaN   1-3-2014
6   789  789.0   1-5-2014
```

To use the final two methods of removing columns, simply create a list of desired columns. Pass that list into the .reindex method or the indexing operation:

```
>>> cols = ['Sales', 'Date']
>>> sales.reindex(columns=cols)
   Sales       Date
0   20.2   1-1-2014
1    8.0   1-2-2014
2   13.0   1-3-2014
3    2.0   1-1-2014
4    3.8   1-2-2014
```

12. Data Frame Methods

```
5    NaN  1-3-2014
6  789.0  1-5-2014
>>> sales[cols]
   Sales      Date
0   20.2  1-1-2014
1    8.0  1-2-2014
2   13.0  1-3-2014
3    2.0  1-1-2014
4    3.8  1-2-2014
5    NaN  1-3-2014
6  789.0  1-5-2014
```

12.9 Slicing

The pandas library provides powerful methods for slicing a data frame. The .head and .tail methods allow for pulling data off the front and end of a data frame. They come in handy when using an interpreter in combination with pandas. By default, they display only the top five or bottom five rows:

```
>>> sales.head()
   UPC Category  Units  Sales      Date
0  1234     Food    5.0   20.2  1-1-2014
1  1234     Food    2.0    8.0  1-2-2014
2  1234     Food    3.0   13.0  1-3-2014
3   789     Food    1.0    2.0  1-1-2014
4   789     Food    2.0    3.8  1-2-2014
```

Simply pass in an integer to override the number of rows to show:

```
>>> sales.tail(2)
   UPC Category  Units  Sales      Date
5  789     Food    NaN    NaN  1-3-2014
6  789     Food    1.0  789.0  1-5-2014
```

Data frames also support slicing based on index position and label. Let's use a string based index so it will be clearer what the slicing options do:

```
>>> sales['new_index'] = list('abcdefg')
>>> df = sales.set_index('new_index')
>>> del sales['new_index']
```

To slice by position, use the .iloc attribute. Here we take rows in positions two up to but not including four:

```
>>> df.iloc[2:4]
           UPC Category  Units  Sales      Date
new_index
c         1234     Food    3.0   13.0  1-3-2014
d          789     Food    1.0    2.0  1-1-2014
```

12.9. Slicing

Row & Column Slicing Examples

```
df.iloc[2:4, 0:1]     ← With a : return data frames
                        Position - Half-open interval
df.loc['d':, 'Units']  ← Without a : return series
                        Label - Closed interval
      Rows    Columns
```

Figure 12.1: Figure showing how to slice by row or column. Note that positional slicing uses the half-open interval, while label based slicing is inclusive (closed interval).

We can also provide column positions that we want to keep as well. The column positions need to follow a comma in the index operation. Here we keep rows from two up to but not including row four. We also take columns from zero up to but not including one (just the column in the zero index position):

```
>>> df.iloc[2:4, 0:1]
           UPC
new_index
c          1234
d          789
```

There is also support for slicing out data by labels. Using the .loc attribute, we can take index values a through d:

```
>>> df.loc['a':'d']
           UPC  Category  Units  Sales      Date
new_index
a          1234  Food      5.0    20.2   1-1-2014
b          1234  Food      2.0     8.0   1-2-2014
c          1234  Food      3.0    13.0   1-3-2014
d          789   Food      1.0     2.0   1-1-2014
```

And just like .iloc, .loc has the ability to specify columns by label. In this example we only take the Units column, and thus it returns a series:

```
>>> df.loc['d':, 'Units']
new_index
d    1.0
e    2.0
f    NaN
g    1.0
Name: Units, dtype: float64
```

119

12. DATA FRAME METHODS

Data Frame Slicing Examples

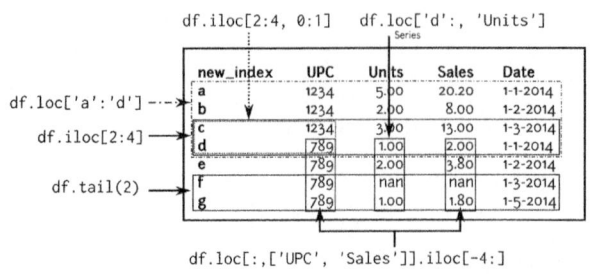

Figure 12.2: Figure showing various ways to slice a data frame. Note that we can slice by label or position.

Below is a summary of the data frame slicing constructs by position and label. To pull out a subset of a data frame using the .iloc or .loc attribute, we do an index operation with cols,rows specifiers, where either specifier is optional.

Note, that when we only want to specify columns, but use all of the rows, we provide a lone : to indicate to slice out all of the rows.

In contrast to normal Python slicing, which are *half-open*, meaning take the start index and go up to, but not including the final index, indexing by labels uses the *closed interval*. A closed interval includes not only the initial location, but also the final location. Indexing by position uses the half-open interval.

The slices are specified by putting a colon between the indices or columns we want to keep. In addition, and again in contrast to Python slicing constructs, you can provide a list of index or column values, if the values are not contiguous.

Slice	Result
.iloc[i:j]	Rows position i up to but not including j (half-open)
.iloc[:,i:j]	Columns position i up to but not including j (half-open)
.iloc[[i,k,m]]	Rows at i, k, and m (not an interval)
.loc[a:b]	Rows from index label a through b (closed)
.loc[:,c:d]	Columns from column label c through d (closed)
.loc[:[b, d, f]]	Columns at labels b, d, and f (not an interval)

120

12.10. Sorting

Hint

If you want to slice out columns by value, but rows by position, you can chain index operations to .iloc or .loc together. Because, the result of the invocation is a data frame or series, we can do further filtering on the result.

Here we pull out columns UPC and Sales, but only the last 4 values:

```
>>> df.loc[:,['UPC', 'Sales']].iloc[-4:]
           UPC    Sales
new_index
d          789    2.0
e          789    3.8
f          789    NaN
g          789    789.0
```

Alternatively, we mentioned avoiding .ix if you can, but this might be a case where you could sneak it in:

```
>>> df.ix[-4:, ['UPC', 'Sales']]
           UPC    Sales
new_index
d          789    2.0
e          789    3.8
f          789    NaN
g          789    789.0
```

12.10 Sorting

Sometimes, we need to sort a data frame by index, or the values in the columns. The data frame operations are very similar to what we saw with series.

Here is the sales data frame:

```
>>> sales
    UPC  Category  Units  Sales      Date
0  1234      Food    5.0   20.2  1-1-2014
1  1234      Food    2.0    8.0  1-2-2014
2  1234      Food    3.0   13.0  1-3-2014
3   789      Food    1.0    2.0  1-1-2014
4   789      Food    2.0    3.8  1-2-2014
5   789      Food    NaN    NaN  1-3-2014
6   789      Food    1.0  789.0  1-5-2014
```

To sort by column, use .sort_values. Let's sort the UPC column:

```
>>> sales.sort_values('UPC')
    UPC  Category  Units  Sales      Date
3   789      Food    1.0    2.0  1-1-2014
4   789      Food    2.0    3.8  1-2-2014
5   789      Food    NaN    NaN  1-3-2014
```

```
6    789     Food    1.0   789.0   1-5-2014
0   1234     Food    5.0    20.2   1-1-2014
1   1234     Food    2.0     8.0   1-2-2014
2   1234     Food    3.0    13.0   1-3-2014
```

Note

Avoid using the .sort method. It is now deprecated, because it does an in-place sort by default. Use .sort_values instead.

The first parameter to .sort_values is the by argument. If we provide a list of columns it will sort by the left-most column first, and then proceed right:

```
>>> sales.sort_values(['Units', 'UPC'])
    UPC  Category  Units   Sales       Date
3   789      Food    1.0     2.0   1-1-2014
6   789      Food    1.0   789.0   1-5-2014
4   789      Food    2.0     3.8   1-2-2014
1  1234      Food    2.0     8.0   1-2-2014
2  1234      Food    3.0    13.0   1-3-2014
0  1234      Food    5.0    20.2   1-1-2014
5   789      Food    NaN     NaN   1-3-2014
```

To sort the index, use the .sort_index method. The index in this data frame is already sorted, so we will sort it in reverse order:

```
>>> sales.sort_index(ascending=False)
    UPC  Category  Units   Sales       Date
6   789      Food    1.0   789.0   1-5-2014
5   789      Food    NaN     NaN   1-3-2014
4   789      Food    2.0     3.8   1-2-2014
3   789      Food    1.0     2.0   1-1-2014
2  1234      Food    3.0    13.0   1-3-2014
1  1234      Food    2.0     8.0   1-2-2014
0  1234      Food    5.0    20.2   1-1-2014
```

12.11 Summary

In this chapter we examined quite a bit of the methods on the DataFrame object. We saw how to examine the data, loop over it, broadcast operations, and serialize it. We also looked at index operations that were very similar to the Series index operations. We saw how to do CRUD operations and ended with slicing and sorting data.

In the next chapter, we will explore some of the statistical functionality found in the data frame.

Chapter 13

Data Frame Statistics

If you are doing data science or statistics with pandas, you are in luck, because the data frame comes with basic functionality built in.

In this section, we will examine snow totals from Alta for the past couple years. I scraped this data off the Utah Avalanche Center website[16], but will use the `.read_table` function of pandas to create a data frame.

```
>>> data = '''year\tinches\tlocation
... 2006\t633.5\tutah
... 2007\t356\tutah
... 2008\t654\tutah
... 2009\t578\tutah
... 2010\t430\tutah
... 2011\t553\tutah
... 2012\t329.5\tutah
... 2013\t382.5\tutah
... 2014\t357.5\tutah
... 2015\t267.5\tutah'''

>>> snow = pd.read_table(StringIO(data))

>>> snow
   year  inches location
0  2006   633.5     utah
1  2007   356.0     utah
2  2008   654.0     utah
3  2009   578.0     utah
4  2010   430.0     utah
5  2011   553.0     utah
6  2012   329.5     utah
7  2013   382.5     utah
8  2014   357.5     utah
9  2015   267.5     utah
```

---

[16]https://utahavalanchecenter.org/alta-monthly-snowfall

13. Data Frame Statistics

13.1 describe and quantile

One of the methods I use a lot is the .describe method. This method provides you with an overview of your data. When I load a new data set, running .describe on it is typically the first thing I do.

With this dataset, the year column, although being numeric, when fed through describe is not too interesting. But, this method is very useful to quickly view the spread of snowfalls over ten years at Alta:

```
>>> snow.describe()
            year       inches
count   10.00000    10.000000
mean  2010.50000   454.150000
std      3.02765   138.357036
min   2006.00000   267.500000
25%   2008.25000   356.375000
50%   2010.50000   406.250000
75%   2012.75000   571.750000
max   2015.00000   654.000000
```

Note that the location column, that has a string type, is ignored by default. If we set the include parameter to 'all', then we also get summary statistics for categorical and string columns:

```
>>> snow.describe(include='all')
            year       inches  location
count   10.00000    10.000000        10
unique       NaN          NaN         1
top          NaN          NaN      utah
freq         NaN          NaN        10
mean  2010.50000   454.150000       NaN
std      3.02765   138.357036       NaN
min   2006.00000   267.500000       NaN
25%   2008.25000   356.375000       NaN
50%   2010.50000   406.250000       NaN
75%   2012.75000   571.750000       NaN
max   2015.00000   654.000000       NaN
```

The .quantile method, by default shows the 50% quantile, though the q parameter can be specified to get different levels:

```
>>> snow.quantile()
year      2010.50
inches     406.25
dtype: float64
```

Here we get the 10% and 90% percentile levels. We can see that if 635 inches fall, we are at the 90% level:

```
>>> snow.quantile(q=[.1, .9])
       year   inches
0.1  2006.9   323.30
0.9  2014.1   635.55
```

13.1. describe and quantile

Note

Changing the q parameter to a list, rather than a scalar, makes the .quantile method return a data frame, rather than a series.

To just get counts of non-empty cells, use the .count method:

```
>>> snow.count()
year         10
inches       10
location     10
dtype: int64
```

If you have data and want to know whether any of the values in the columns evaluate to True in a boolean context, use the .any method:

```
>>> snow.any()
year         True
inches       True
location     True
dtype: bool
```

This method can also be applied to a row, by using the axis=1 parameter:

```
>>> snow.any(axis=1)
0    True
1    True
2    True
3    True
4    True
5    True
6    True
7    True
8    True
9    True
dtype: bool
```

Likewise, there is a corresponding .all method to indicate whether all of the values are *truthy*:

```
>>> snow.all()
year         True
inches       True
location     True
dtype: bool
```

```
>>> snow.all(axis=1)
0    True
1    True
2    True
3    True
```

125

13. Data Frame Statistics

```
4       True
5       True
6       True
7       True
8       True
9       True
dtype: bool
```

Both .any and .all are pretty boring in this data set because they are all truthy (non-empty or not false).

13.2 rank

The .rank method goes through every column and assigns a number to the rank of that cell within the column. Again, the year column isn't particularly useful here:

```
>>> snow.rank()
   year  inches  location
0   1.0     9.0       5.5
1   2.0     3.0       5.5
2   3.0    10.0       5.5
3   4.0     8.0       5.5
4   5.0     6.0       5.5
5   6.0     7.0       5.5
6   7.0     2.0       5.5
7   8.0     5.0       5.5
8   9.0     4.0       5.5
9  10.0     1.0       5.5
```

Because the default behavior is to rank by ascending order, this might be the wrong order for snowfall (unless you are ranking worst snowfall). To fix this, set the ascending parameter to False:

```
>>> snow.rank(ascending=False)
   year  inches  location
0  10.0     2.0       5.5
1   9.0     8.0       5.5
2   8.0     1.0       5.5
3   7.0     3.0       5.5
4   6.0     5.0       5.5
5   5.0     4.0       5.5
6   4.0     9.0       5.5
7   3.0     6.0       5.5
8   2.0     7.0       5.5
9   1.0    10.0       5.5
```

Note that because the location columns are all the same, the rank of that column is the average by default. To change this behavior, we can set the method parameter to 'min', 'max', 'first', or 'dense' to get the lowest, highest, order of appearance, or ranking by group (instead of items) respectively ('average' is the default):

```
>>> snow.rank(method='min')
   year  inches  location
0   1.0     9.0       1.0
1   2.0     3.0       1.0
2   3.0    10.0       1.0
3   4.0     8.0       1.0
4   5.0     6.0       1.0
5   6.0     7.0       1.0
6   7.0     2.0       1.0
7   8.0     5.0       1.0
8   9.0     4.0       1.0
9  10.0     1.0       1.0
```

Note

Specifying method='first' fails with non-numeric data:

```
>>> snow.rank(method='first')
Traceback (most recent call last):
  ...
ValueError: first not supported for non-numeric data
```

13.3 clip

Occasionally, there are outliers in the data. If this is problematic, the .clip method trims a column (or row if axis=1) to certain values:

```
>>> snow.clip(lower=400, upper=600)
Traceback (most recent call last):
  ...
TypeError: unorderable types: str() >= int()
```

For our data, clipping fails as location is a column containing string types. Unless your columns are semi-homogenous, you might want to run the .clip method on the individual series or the subset of columns that need to be clipped:

```
>>> snow[['inches']].clip(lower=400, upper=600)
   inches
0   600.0
1   400.0
2   600.0
3   578.0
4   430.0
5   553.0
6   400.0
7   400.0
8   400.0
9   400.0
```

13.4 Correlation and Covariance

We've already seen that the series object can perform a Pearson correlation with another series. The data frame offers similar functionality, but it will do a *pairwise* correlation with all of the numeric columns. In addition, it will perform a Kendall or Spearman correlation, when those strings are passed to the optional method parameter:

```
>>> snow.corr()
            year     inches
year    1.000000  -0.698064
inches -0.698064   1.000000

>>> snow.corr(method='spearman')
            year     inches
year    1.000000  -0.648485
inches -0.648485   1.000000
```

If you have two data frames that you want to correlate, you can use the .corrwith method to compute column-wise (the default) or row-wise (when axis=1) Pearson correlations:

```
>>> snow2 = snow[['inches']] - 100
>>> snow.corrwith(snow2)
inches   1.0
year     NaN
dtype: float64
```

The .cov method of the data frame computes the pair-wise covariance (non-normalized correlation):

```
>>> snow.cov()
             year         inches
year     9.166667    -292.416667
inches -292.416667  19142.669444
```

13.5 Reductions

There are various *reducing* methods on the data frame, that collapse columns into a single value. An example is the .sum method, which will apply the add operation to all members of columns. Note, that by default, string columns are concatenated:

```
>>> snow.sum()
year                                                  20105
inches                                               4541.5
location    utahutahutahutahutahutahutahutahutahutah
dtype: object
```

13.5. Reductions

If you prefer only numeric sums, use `numeric_only=True` parameter:

```
>>> snow.sum(numeric_only=True)
year      20105.0
inches     4541.5
dtype: float64
```

To apply a multiplicative reduction, use the `.prod` method. Note that the product ignores non-numeric rows:

```
>>> snow.prod()
year      1.079037e+33
inches    2.443332e+26
dtype: float64
```

The `.describe` method is the workhorse for quickly summarizing tables of data. If you need the individual measures, pandas provides those as well. This method includes: count, mean, standard deviation, minimum, 25% quantile, median, 75% quantile, and maximum value. Their corresponding methods are `.count`, `.mean`, `.std`, `.min`, `.quantile(q=.25)`, `.median`, `quantile(q=.75)`, and `.max`.

One nicety of these individual methods is that you can pass `axis=1` to get the reduction across the rows, rather than the columns:

```
>>> snow.mean()
year      2010.50
inches     454.15
dtype: float64

>>> snow.mean(axis=1)
0    1319.75
1    1181.50
2    1331.00
3    1293.50
4    1220.00
5    1282.00
6    1170.75
7    1197.75
8    1185.75
9    1141.25
dtype: float64
```

Variance is a measure that is not included in the `.describe` method output. However, this calculation is available as a method named `.var`:

```
>>> snow.var()
year          9.166667
inches    19142.669444
dtype: float64
```

13. Data Frame Statistics

Other measures for describing dispersion and distributions are .mad, .skew, and .kurt, for mean absolute deviation, skew, and kurtosis respectively:

```
>>> snow.mad()
year        2.50
inches    120.38
dtype: float64

>>> snow.skew()
year      0.000000
inches    0.311866
dtype: float64

>>> snow.kurt()
year     -1.200000
inches   -1.586098
dtype: float64
```

As mentioned, the maximum and minimum values are provided by describe. If you prefer to know the index of those values, you can use the .idxmax and .idxmin methods respectively. Note that these fail with non-numeric columns:

```
>>> snow.idxmax()
Traceback (most recent call last):
  ...
ValueError: could not convert string to float: 'utah'

>>> snow[['year', 'inches']].idxmax()
year      9
inches    2
dtype: int64
```

13.6 Summary

The pandas library provides basic statistical operations out of the box. This chapter looked at the .describe method, which is one of the first tools I reach for when looking at new data. We also saw how to sort data, clip it to certain ranges, perform correlations, and reduce columns.

In the next chapter, we will look at the more advanced topics of changing the shape of the data.

Chapter 14

Grouping, Pivoting, and Reshaping

One of the more advanced features of pandas is the ability to perform operations on *groups* of data frames. That is a little abstract, but power users from Excel are familiar with *pivot tables*, and pandas gives us this same functionality.

For this section we will use data representing student scores:

```
>>> scores = pd.DataFrame({
...     'name':['Adam', 'Bob', 'Dave', 'Fred'],
...     'age': [15, 16, 16, 15],
...     'test1': [95, 81, 89, None],
...     'test2': [80, 82, 84, 88],
...     'teacher': ['Ashby', 'Ashby', 'Jones', 'Jones']})
```

The data looks like this:

name	age	test1	test2	teacher
Adam	15	95	80	Ashby
Bob	16	81	82	Ashby
Dave	16	89	84	Jones
Fred	15		88	Jones

Note that Fred is missing a score from test1. That could represent that he did not take the test, or that someone forget to enter his score.

14.1 Reducing Methods in groupby

The lower level workhorse that provides the ability to group data frames by column values, then merge them back into a result is the .groupby method. As an example, on the scores data frame, we will

14. GROUPING, PIVOTING, AND RESHAPING

Groupby Split Apply Combine

	age	name	teacher	test1	test2
0	15	Adam	Ashby	95.00	80
1	16	Bob	Ashby	81.00	82
2	16	Dave	Jones	89.00	84
3	15	Fred	Jones	nan	88

Split

groups = df.groupby('teacher')

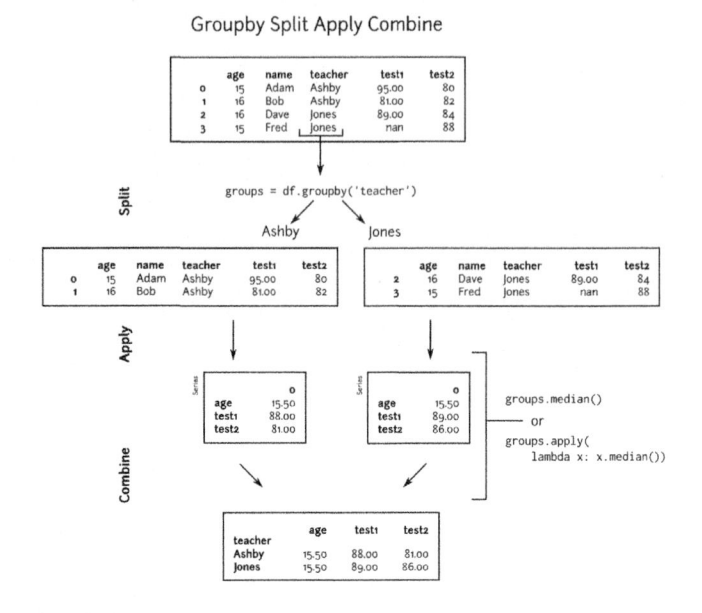

Ashby

	age	name	teacher	test1	test2
0	15	Adam	Ashby	95.00	80
1	16	Bob	Ashby	81.00	82

Jones

	age	name	teacher	test1	test2
2	16	Dave	Jones	89.00	84
3	15	Fred	Jones	nan	88

Apply

	0
age	15.50
test1	88.00
test2	81.00

	0
age	15.50
test1	89.00
test2	86.00

groups.median()
or
groups.apply(
  lambda x: x.median())

Combine

teacher	age	test1	test2
Ashby	15.50	88.00	81.00
Jones	15.50	89.00	86.00

Figure 14.1: Figure showing the split, apply, and combine steps on a groupby object. Note that there are various built-in methods, and also the `apply` method, which allows arbitrary operations.

compute the median scores for each teacher. First we call `.groupby` and then invoke `.median` on the result:

```
>>> scores.groupby('teacher').median()
         age   test1   test2
teacher
Ashby    15.5  88.0    81.0
Jones    15.5  89.0    86.0
```

This included the age column, to ignore that we can slice out just the test columns:

```
>>> scores.groupby('teacher').median()[['test1', 'test2']]
         test1   test2
teacher
Ashby    88.0    81.0
Jones    89.0    86.0
```

The result of calling `.groupby` is a `GroupBy` object. In this case, the object has grouped all the rows with the same teach together. Calling

14.1. Reducing Methods in groupby

`.median` on the GroupBy object returns a new `DataFrame` object that has the median score for each teacher group.

Grouping can be very powerful, and you can use multiple columns to group by as well. To find the median values for every age group for each teacher, simply group by teacher and age:

```
>>> scores.groupby(['teacher', 'age']).median()
             test1   test2
teacher age
Ashby   15    95.0      80
        16    81.0      82
Jones   15     NaN      88
        16    89.0      84
```

Note

When you group by multiple columns, the result has a hierarchical index or *multi-level index*.

If we want both the minimum and maximum test scores by teacher, we use the .agg method and pass in a list of functions to call:

```
>>> scores.groupby(['teacher', 'age']).agg([min, max])
              name         test1         test2
               min   max    min   max    min max
teacher age
Ashby   15    Adam  Adam   95.0  95.0     80  80
        16     Bob   Bob   81.0  81.0     82  82
Jones   15    Fred  Fred    NaN   NaN     88  88
        16    Dave  Dave   89.0  89.0     84  84
```

The groupby object has many methods that reduce group values to a single value, they are:

133

14. Grouping, Pivoting, and Reshaping

Method	Result
`.all`	Boolean if all cells in group are `True`
`.any`	Boolean if any cells in group are `True`
`.count`	Count of non null values
`.size`	Size of group (includes null)
`.idxmax`	Index of maximum values
`.idxmin`	Index of minimum values
`.quantile`	Quantile (default of .5) of group
`.agg(func)`	Apply func to each group. If func returns scalar, then reducing
`.apply(func)`	Use split-apply-combine rules
`.last`	Last value
`.nth`	Nth row from group
`.max`	Maximum value
`.min`	Minimum value
`.mean`	Mean value
`.median`	Median value
`.sem`	Standard error of mean of group
`.std`	Standard deviation
`.var`	Variation of group
`.prod`	Product of group
`.sum`	Sum of group

14.2 Pivot Tables

Using a pivot table, we can generalize certain groupby behaviors. To get the median teacher scores we can run the following:

```
>>> scores.pivot_table(index='teacher',
...       values=['test1', 'test2'],
...       aggfunc='median')
         test1  test2
teacher
Ashby     88.0     81
Jones     89.0     86
```

If we want to aggregate by teacher and age, we simply use a list with both of them for the index parameter:

```
>>> scores.pivot_table(index=['teacher', 'age'],
...       values=['test1', 'test2'],
...       aggfunc='median')
             test1  test2
teacher age
Ashby   15    95.0     80
        16    81.0     82
Jones   15     NaN     88
        16    89.0     84
```

If we want to apply multiple functions, just use a list of them. Here, we look at the minimum and maximum test scores by teacher:

14.2. Pivot Tables

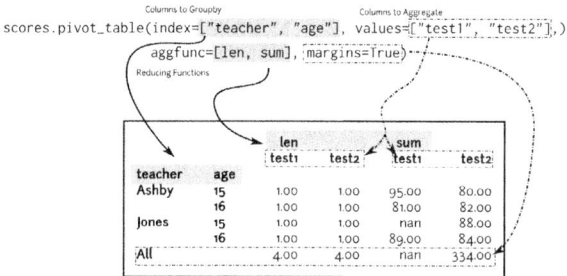

Figure 14.2: Figure showing different parameters provided to `pivot_table` method.

```
>>> scores.pivot_table(index='teacher',
...     values=['test1', 'test2'],
...     aggfunc=[min, max])
           min         max
         test1 test2 test1 test2
teacher
Ashby    81.0    80  95.0    82
Jones    89.0    84  89.0    88
```

We can see that pivot table and group by behavior is very similar. Many spreadsheet power users are more familiar with the declarative style of `.pivot_table`, while programmers not accustomed to pivot tables prefer using group by semantics.

One additional feature of pivot tables is the ability to add summary rows. Simply by setting margins=True we get this functionality:

```
>>> scores.pivot_table(index='teacher',
...     values=['test1', 'test2'],
...     aggfunc='median', margins=True)
         test1  test2
teacher
Ashby    88.0   81.0
Jones    89.0   86.0
All      89.0   83.0
```

135

14. Grouping, Pivoting, and Reshaping

Pivot Table Examples

	age	name	teacher	test1	test2
0	15	Adam	Ashby	95.00	80
1	16	Bob	Ashby	81.00	82
2	16	Dave	Jones	89.00	84
3	15	Fred	Jones	nan	88

☐ ○ △

teacher	test1	test2
Ashby	88.00	81
Jones	89.00	86

☐ ○ △ ☆

teacher	test1	test2
Ashby	88.00	81.00
Jones	89.00	86.00
All	89.00	83.00

.pivot_table **options**

☐ index="teacher"
■ index=["teacher", "age"]
○ aggfunc="median"
● aggfunc=[min, max]
△ values=["test1", "test2"]
☆ margins=True

■ ○ △

teacher	age	test1	test2
Ashby	15	95.00	80
	16	81.00	82
Jones	15	nan	88
	16	89.00	84

☐ ● △

		min		max	
teacher	test1	test2	test1	test2
Ashby	81.00	80	95.00	82
Jones	89.00	84	89.00	88

Figure 14.3: Figure showing results of different parameters provided to `pivot_table` method.

14.3 Melting Data

In OLAP terms, there is a notion of a *fact* and a *dimension*. A fact is a value that is measured and reported on. A dimension is a group of values the describe the conditions of the fact. In a sales scenario, typical facts would be the number of sales of an item and the cost of the item. The dimensions might be the store where the item was sold, the date, and the customer.

The dimensions can then be *sliced* to dissect the data. We might want to view sales by store. A dimension may be hierarchical, a store could have a region, zip code, or state. We could view sales by any of those dimensions.

The scores data is in a *wide* format (sometimes called *stacked* or *record* form). In contrast to a "long" format (sometimes called *tidy* form), where each row contains a single fact (with perhaps other variables describing the dimensions). If we consider test score to be a fact, this wide format has more than one fact in a row, hence it is wide.

Often, tools require that data be stored in a long format, and only have one fact per row. This format is *denormalized* and repeats many of the dimensions, but makes analysis easier.

Our wide version looks like:

14.3. Melting Data

name	age	test1	test2	teacher
Adam	15	95	80	Ashby
Bob	16	81	82	Ashby
Dave	16	89	84	Jones
Fred	15		88	Jones

A long version of our scores might look like this:

name	age	test	score
Adam	15	test1	95
Bob	16	test1	81
Dave	16	test1	89
Fred	15	test1	NaN
Adam	15	test2	80
Bob	16	test2	82
Dave	16	test2	84
Fred	15	test2	88

Using the `melt` function in pandas, we can tweak the data so it becomes long. Since I am used to OLAP parlance (facts and dimensions), I will use those terms to explain how to use `melt`.

In the scores data frame, we have facts in the test1 and test2 column. We want to have a new data frame, where the test name is pulled out into its own column, and the scores for the test are in a single column. To do this, we put the list of fact columns in the value_vars parameter. Any dimensions we want to keep should be listed in the id_vars parameter.

Here we keep name and age as dimensions, and pull out the test scores as facts:

```
>>> pd.melt(scores, id_vars=['name', 'age'],
...         value_vars=['test1', 'test2'])
   name  age variable  value
0  Adam   15    test1   95.0
1   Bob   16    test1   81.0
2  Dave   16    test1   89.0
3  Fred   15    test1    NaN
4  Adam   15    test2   80.0
5   Bob   16    test2   82.0
6  Dave   16    test2   84.0
7  Fred   15    test2   88.0
```

If we want to change the description of the fact from variable to a more descriptive name, pass that as the var_name parameter. To change the name of the fact column (it defaults to value), use the value_name parameter:

```
>>> pd.melt(scores, id_vars=['name', 'age'],
...         value_vars=['test1', 'test2'],
```

137

14. Grouping, Pivoting, and Reshaping

Melting Data

	age	name	teacher	test1	test2
0	15	Adam	Ashby	95.00	80
1	16	Bob	Ashby	81.00	82
2	16	Dave	Jones	89.00	84
3	15	Fred	Jones	nan	88

pd.melt(scores, id_vars=['name', 'age'], value_vars=['test1', 'test2'])

Denormalized Data   Column names (var_name)   Column values (value_name)

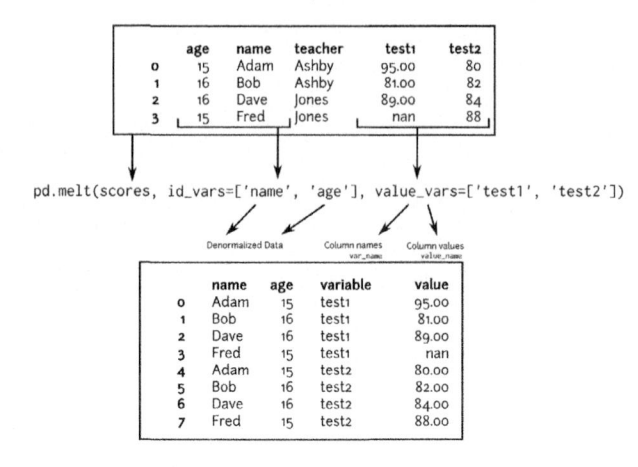

	name	age	variable	value
0	Adam	15	test1	95.00
1	Bob	16	test1	81.00
2	Dave	16	test1	89.00
3	Fred	15	test1	nan
4	Adam	15	test2	80.00
5	Bob	16	test2	82.00
6	Dave	16	test2	84.00
7	Fred	15	test2	88.00

Figure 14.4: Figure showing columns that are preserved during melting, id_vars, and column names that are pulled into columns, value_vars.

```
...            var_name='test', value_name='score')
    name  age   test   score
0   Adam   15  test1    95.0
1    Bob   16  test1    81.0
2   Dave   16  test1    89.0
3   Fred   15  test1     NaN
4   Adam   15  test2    80.0
5    Bob   16  test2    82.0
6   Dave   16  test2    84.0
7   Fred   15  test2    88.0
```

Note

Long data is also referred to as *tidy* data. See the Tidy Data paper[17] by Hadley Wickham.

14.4 Converting Back to Wide

Using a pivot table, we can go from long format to wide format. It is a little more involved going in the reverse direction:

```
>>> long_df = pd.melt(scores, id_vars=['name', 'age'],
...          value_vars=['test1', 'test2'],
...          var_name='test', value_name='score')
```

First, we pivot, using the dimensions as the `index` parameter, the name of the fact column name as the `columns` parameter, and the fact column as the `values` parameter:

```
>>> wide_df = long_df.pivot_table(index=['name', 'age'],
...     columns=['test'],
...     values=['score'])
>>> wide_df
          score
test      test1 test2
name age
Adam 15   95.0  80.0
Bob  16   81.0  82.0
Dave 16   89.0  84.0
Fred 15   NaN   88.0
```

Note that this creates *hierarchical column labels*, (or *multi-level*) and *hierarchical index*. To flatten the index, use the `.reset_index` method. It will take the existing index, and make a column (or columns if it is hierarchical):

```
>>> wide_df = wide_df.reset_index()
>>> wide_df
       name age score
test            test1 test2
0      Adam 15  95.0  80.0
1      Bob  16  81.0  82.0
2      Dave 16  89.0  84.0
3      Fred 15  NaN   88.0
```

To flatten the nested columns, we can use the `.get_level_values` method from the `column` attribute. This is a little trickier, because we want to merge into the level 1 columns the values from level 0, if

---

[17]http://vita.had.co.nz/papers/tidy-data.html

14. Grouping, Pivoting, and Reshaping

level 1 is the empty string. I'm going to use a *conditional expression* inside of a *list comprehension* to do the job:

```
>>> cols = wide_df.columns
>>> cols.get_level_values(0)
Index(['name', 'age', 'score', 'score'], dtype='object')

>>> cols.get_level_values(1)
Index(['', '', 'test1', 'test2'], dtype='object', name='test')

>>> l1 = cols.get_level_values(1)
>>> l0 = cols.get_level_values(0)
>>> names = [x[1] if x[1] else x[0] for x in zip(l0, l1)]
>>> names
['name', 'age', 'test1', 'test2']
```

Finally, set the new names as the column names:

```
>>> wide_df.columns = names
>>> wide_df
   name  age  test1  test2
0  Adam   15   95.0   80.0
1   Bob   16   81.0   82.0
2  Dave   16   89.0   84.0
3  Fred   15    NaN   88.0
```

14.5 Creating Dummy Variables

A *dummy variable* (sometimes known as an indicator variable) is a variable that has a value of 1 or 0. This variable typically indicates whether the presence or absence of a categorical feature is found. For example, in the scores data frame, we have an age column. Some systems might prefer to have a column for every age (15 and 16 in this case), with a 1 or 0 to indicate whether the row has that age. This can create pretty sparse matrixes if there are many categories.

Many machine learning models require that their input be crafted in this way. As pandas is often used to prep data for models, let's see how to do it with the age column. The get_dummies function provides what we need:

```
>>> pd.get_dummies(scores, columns=['age'], prefix='age')
   name teacher  test1  test2  age_15  age_16
0  Adam   Ashby   95.0     80     1.0     0.0
1   Bob   Ashby   81.0     82     0.0     1.0
2  Dave   Jones   89.0     84     0.0     1.0
3  Fred   Jones    NaN     88     1.0     0.0
```

The columns parameter refers to a list (note a single string will fail) of columns we want to change into dummy columns. The prefix parameter specifies what we want to prefix each of the category values with when they are turned into column names.

14.6 Undoing Dummy Variables

Creating dummy variables is easy. Undoing them is harder. Here is a function that will undo it:

```
>>> def undummy(df, prefix, new_col_name, val_type=float):
...     ''' df - dataframe with dummy columns
...         prefix - prefix of dummy columns
...         new_col_name - column name to replace dummy columns
...         val_type - callable type for new column
...     '''
...     dummy_cols = [col for col in df.columns
...                   if col.startswith(prefix)]
...
...     # map of index location of dummy variable to new value
...     idx2val = {i:val_type(col[len(prefix):]) for i, col
...                in enumerate(dummy_cols)}
...
...     def get_index(vals): # idx of dummy col to use
...         return list(vals).index(1)
...
...     # using the dummy_cols lookup the new value by idx
...     ser = df[dummy_cols].apply(
...         lambda x: idx2val.get(get_index(x), None), axis=1)
...     df[new_col_name] = ser
...     df = df.drop(dummy_cols, axis=1)
...     return df
>>> dum = pd.get_dummies(scores, columns=['age'], prefix='age')
>>> undummy(dum, 'age_', 'age')
   name teacher  test1  test2   age
0  Adam   Ashby   95.0     80  15.0
1   Bob   Ashby   81.0     82  16.0
2  Dave   Jones   89.0     84  16.0
3  Fred   Jones    NaN     88  15.0
```

14.7 Stacking and Unstacking

Another mechanism to tweak data is to "stack" and "unstack" it. This is particularly useful when you have multi-level indices, which you get from pivot tables if you pass in a list for the `index` parameter.

Unstacking takes a dataset that has a multi-level index and pulls out the inner most level of the index and makes it the inner most level the columns. Stacking does the reverse. See the image for a visual example.

14.8 Summary

This chapter covered some more advanced topics of pandas. We saw how to group by columns and perform reductions. We also saw how some of these group by operations can be done with the

14. GROUPING, PIVOTING, AND RESHAPING

Stacking/Unstacking

	age	name	teacher	test1	test2
0	15	Adam	Ashby	95.00	80
1	16	Bob	Ashby	81.00	82
2	16	Dave	Jones	89.00	84
3	15	Fred	Jones	nan	88

```
df.groupby(['teacher', 'age']).min()
```

teacher	age	name	test1	test2
Ashby	15	Adam	95.00	80
	16	Bob	81.00	82
Jones	15	Fred	nan	88
	16	Dave	89.00	84

unstack — Innermost index labels
stack — Innermost column labels

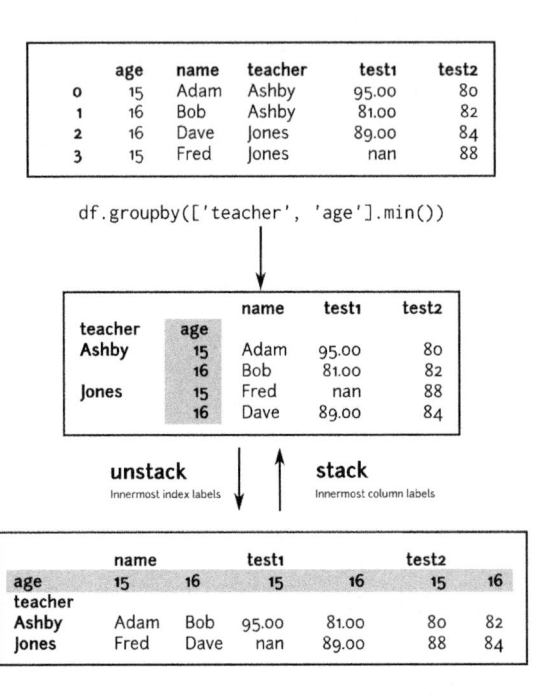

	name		test1		test2	
age	15	16	15	16	15	16
teacher						
Ashby	Adam	Bob	95.00	81.00	80	82
Jones	Fred	Dave	nan	89.00	88	84

Figure 14.5: Figure showing how to stack and unstack data. Stack takes the innermost column label and places them in the index. Unstack takes the innermost index labels and places them in the columns.

14.8. Summary

.pivot_table method. Then we looked at *melting* data, creating dummy variables, and stacking.

Often, we you find you need your data organized slightly differently, you can use one of these tools to re-arrange it for you. It will be quicker, and have less code than an imperative solution requiring iterating over the values manually. But, it might require a little while pondering how to transform the data. Play around with these methods and check out other examples of how people are using them in the wild for inspiration.

Chapter 15

Dealing With Missing Data

More often than I would like, I spend time being a data janitor. Cleaning up, removing, updating, and tweaking data I need to deal with. This can be annoying, but luckily pandas has good support for these actions. We've already seen much of this type of work. In this section we will discuss dealing with missing data.

Let's start out by looking a simple data frame with missing data. I'll use the `StringIO` class and the pandas `read_table` function to simulate reading tabular data:

```
>>> import io
>>> data = '''Name|Age|Color
... Fred|22|Red
... Sally|29|Blue
... George|24|
... Fido||Black'''

>>> df = pd.read_table(io.StringIO(data), sep='|')
```

This data is missing some values:

```
>>> df
     Name   Age  Color
0    Fred  22.0    Red
1   Sally  29.0   Blue
2  George  24.0    NaN
3    Fido   NaN  Black
```

Data can be missing for many reasons. Here are a few, though there are more:

- User error - User did not enter data
- Programming error - Logic drops data

15. Dealing With Missing Data

- Integration error - When integrating data systems, syncing is broken

- Hardware issues - Storage devices out of space

- Measurement error - When measuring amounts, there might be a difference between 0 and a lack of measurement

Perhaps more insidious is when you are missing (a big chunk of) data and don't even notice it. I've found that plotting can be a useful tool to visually see holes in the data. Below we will discuss a few more.

In our df data, one might assume that there should be an age for every row. Every living thing has an age, but Fido's is missing. Is that because he didn't want anyone to know how old he was? Maybe he doesn't know his birthday? Maybe he isn't a human, so giving him an age doesn't make sense. To effectively deal with missing data, it is useful to determine which data is missing and why it is missing. This will aid in deciding what to do with the missing data. Unfortunately, this book can not help with that. That requires sleuthing and often non-programming related skills.

15.1 Finding Missing Data

The .isnull method of a data frame returns a data frame filled with boolean values. The cells are True where the data is missing:

```
>>> df.isnull()
    Name    Age   Color
0  False  False   False
1  False  False   False
2  False  False    True
3  False   True   False
```

With our small dataset we can visually inspect that there is missing data. With larger datasets of many columns and perhaps millions of rows, inspection doesn't work as well. Applying the .any method to the result will give you a series that has the column names as index labels and boolean values that indicate whether a column has missing values:

```
>>> df.isnull().any()
Name     False
Age       True
Color     True
dtype: bool
```

15.2 Dropping Missing Data

Dropping rows with missing data is straightforward. To drop any row that is missing data, simply use the .dropna method:

```
>>> df.dropna()
    Name   Age  Color
0   Fred   22.0   Red
1   Sally  29.0  Blue
```

To be more selective, we can use the result of .notnull. This is the complement of .isnull. With this data frame in hand, we can simply choose which column to mask by. We can remove missing ages. Note that the column type of Age will be a float and not an integer type, even after we removed the NaN that caused the coercion to float in the first place:

```
>>> valid = df.notnull()
>>> df[valid.Age]
    Name    Age   Color
0   Fred    22.0    Red
1   Sally   29.0   Blue
2   George  24.0    NaN
```

Or we can get rows for valid colors by filtering with the Color column of the valid data frame:

```
>>> df[valid.Color]
    Name   Age   Color
0   Fred   22.0    Red
1   Sally  29.0   Blue
3   Fido   NaN   Black
```

What if you wanted to get the rows that were valid for both age and color? You could combine the column masks using a boolean and operator (&):

```
>>> mask = valid.Age & valid.Color
>>> mask
0    True
1    True
2    False
3    False
dtype: bool

>>> df[mask]
    Name   Age  Color
0   Fred   22.0   Red
1   Sally  29.0  Blue
```

In this case, the result is the same as .dropna, but in other cases it might be ok to keep missing values around in certain columns. When that need arises, .dropna is too heavy-handed, and you will need to be a little more fine grained with your mask.

15. Dealing With Missing Data

Note

In pandas, there is often more than one way to do something. Another option to combine the two column masks would be like this. Use the .apply method on the columns with the Python built-in function all. To collapse these boolean values along the row, make sure you pass the axis=1 parameter:

```
>>> mask = valid[['Age', 'Color']].apply(all, axis=1)
>>> mask
0     True
1     True
2    False
3    False
dtype: bool
```

In general, I try to prefer the simplest method. In this case, that is the & operator. If you needed to apply a user defined function across the row to determine if a row is valid, then .apply would be a better choice.

15.3 Inserting Data for Missing Data

Continuing on with this data, we will examine methods to fill in the missing data. Below is the data frame:

```
>>> df
     Name   Age  Color
0    Fred  22.0    Red
1   Sally  29.0   Blue
2  George  24.0    NaN
3    Fido   NaN  Black
```

The easiest method to replace missing data is via the .fillna method. With a scalar argument it will replace all missing data with that value:

```
>>> df.fillna('missing')
     Name      Age    Color
0    Fred       22      Red
1   Sally       29     Blue
2  George       24  missing
3    Fido  missing    Black
```

To specify values on a per column basis, pass in a dictionary to .fillna:

```
>>> df.fillna({'Age': df.Age.median(),
...            'Color': 'Pink'})
     Name   Age  Color
0    Fred  22.0    Red
1   Sally  29.0   Blue
```

15.3. Inserting Data for Missing Data

```
2  George  24.0   Pink
3    Fido  24.0  Black
```

An alternate method of replacing missing data is to use the fillna method with either ffill or bfill. These options do either a *forward fill* (take the value before the missing value) or *backwards fill* (use the value after the missing value) respectively:

```
>>> df.fillna(method='ffill')
     Name   Age  Color
0    Fred  22.0    Red
1   Sally  29.0   Blue
2  George  24.0   Blue
3    Fido  24.0  Black

>>> df.fillna(method='bfill')
     Name   Age  Color
0    Fred  22.0    Red
1   Sally  29.0   Blue
2  George  24.0  Black
3    Fido   NaN  Black
```

Note

A ffill of bfill is not guaranteed to insert data if the first or last value is missing. The .fillna call with bfill above illustrates this.

This is a small example of an operation that you cannot blindly apply to a dataset. Just because it worked on a past dataset, it is not a guarantee that it will work on a future dataset.

If your data is organized row-wise then providing axis=1 will fill along the row axis:

```
>>> df.fillna(method='ffill', axis=1)
     Name   Age  Color
0    Fred    22    Red
1   Sally    29   Blue
2  George    24     24
3    Fido  Fido  Black
```

If you have numeric data that has some ordering, then another option is the .interpolate method. This will fill in values based on the method parameter provided:

```
>>> df.interpolate()
     Name   Age  Color
0    Fred  22.0    Red
1   Sally  29.0   Blue
2  George  24.0    NaN
3    Fido  24.0  Black
```

15. Dealing With Missing Data

Below are tables describing the different interpolate options for method:

Method	Effect
linear	Treat values as evenly spaced (default)
time	Fill in values based in based on time index
values/index	Use the index to fill in blanks

If you have scipy installed you can use the following additional options:

Method	Effect
nearest	Use nearest data point
zero	Zero order spline (use last value seen)
slinear	Spline interpolation of first order
quadratic	Spline interpolation of second order
cubic	Spline interpolation of third order
polynomial	Polynomial interpolation (pass order param)
spline	Spline interpolation (pass order param)
barycentric	Use Barycentric Lagrange Interpolation
krogh	Use Krogh Interpolation
piecewise_polynomial	Use Piecewise Polynomial Interpolation
pchip	Use Piecewise Cubic Hermite Interpolating Polynomial

Finally, you can use the .replace method to fill in missing values:

```
>>> df.replace(np.nan, value=-1)
    Name   Age  Color
0   Fred  22.0    Red
1  Sally  29.0   Blue
2 George  24.0     -1
3   Fido  -1.0  Black
```

Note that if you try to replace None, pandas will throw an error, as this is the default value for the value parameter:

```
>>> df.replace(None, value=-1)
Traceback (most recent call last):
 ...
TypeError: 'regex' must be a string or a compiled regular
expression or a list or dict of strings or regular expressions,
you passed a 'bool'
```

15.4 Summary

In the real world data is messy. Sometimes you have to tweak it slightly or filter it. And sometimes, it is just missing. In these cases, having insight into your data and where it came from is invaluable.

In this chapter we saw how to find missing data. We saw how to simply drop that data that is incomplete. We also saw methods for filling in the missing data.

Chapter 16

Joining Data Frames

Data frames hold tabular data. Databases hold tabular data. You can perform many of the same operations on data frames that you do to database tables. In this section we will examine joining data frames.

Here are the two tables we will examine:

Index	color	name
0	Blue	John
1	Blue	George
2	Purple	Ringo

Index	carcolor	name
3	Red	Paul
1	Blue	George
2		Ringo

16.1 Adding Rows to Data Frames

Let's assume that we have two data frames that we want to combine into a single data frame, with rows from both. The simplest way to do this is with the concat function. Below, we create two data frames:

```
>>> df1 = pd.DataFrame({'name': ['John', 'George', 'Ringo'],
...                     'color': ['Blue', 'Blue', 'Purple']})
>>> df2 = pd.DataFrame({'name': ['Paul', 'George', 'Ringo'],
...                     'carcolor': ['Red', 'Blue', np.nan]},
...                    index=[3, 1, 2])
```

153

16. JOINING DATA FRAMES

The concat function in the pandas library accepts a list of data frames to combine. It will find any columns that have the same name, and use a single column for each of the repeated columns. In this case name is common to both data frames:

```
>>> pd.concat([df1, df2])
   carcolor   color    name
0       NaN    Blue    John
1       NaN    Blue  George
2       NaN  Purple   Ringo
3       Red     NaN    Paul
1      Blue     NaN  George
2       NaN     NaN   Ringo
```

Note that .concat preserves index values, so the resulting data frame has duplicate index values. If you would prefer an error when duplicates appear, you can pass the verify_integrity=True parameter setting:

```
>>> pd.concat([df1, df2], verify_integrity=True)
Traceback (most recent call last):
  ...
ValueError: Indexes have overlapping values: [1, 2]
```

Alternatively, if you would prefer that pandas create new index values for you, pass in ignore_index=True as a parameter:

```
>>> pd.concat([df1, df2], ignore_index=True)
   carcolor   color    name
0       NaN    Blue    John
1       NaN    Blue  George
2       NaN  Purple   Ringo
3       Red     NaN    Paul
4      Blue     NaN  George
5       NaN     NaN   Ringo
```

16.2 Adding Columns to Data Frames

The concat function also has the ability to align data frames based on index values, rather than using the columns. By passing axis=1, we get this behavior:

```
>>> pd.concat([df1, df2], axis=1)
   color    name  carcolor    name
0   Blue    John       NaN     NaN
1   Blue  George      Blue  George
2 Purple   Ringo       NaN   Ringo
3    NaN     NaN       Red    Paul
```

Note that this repeats the name column. Using SQL, we can *join* two database tables together based on common columns. If we want

154

16.3. Joins

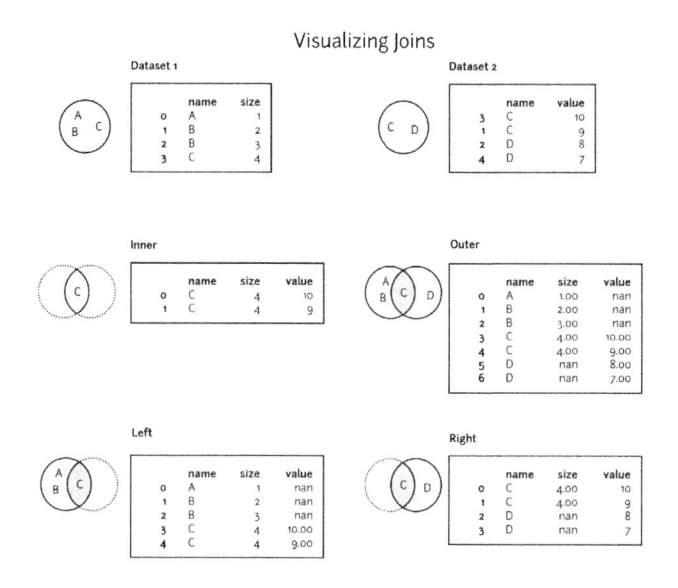

Figure 16.1: Figure showing how the result of four different joins: inner, outer, left, and right.

to perform a join like a database join on data frames, we need to use the .merge method. We will cover that in the next section.

16.3 Joins

Databases have different types of joins. The four common ones include inner, outer, left, and right. The data frame has a method to support these operations. Sadly, it is not the .join method, but rather the .merge method.

> **Note**
>
> The .join method is meant for joining based on index, rather than columns. In practice I find myself joining based on columns instead of index values.
>
> To use the .join method to join based on column values, you need to set that column as the index first:
>
> ```
> >>> df1.set_index('name').join(df2.set_index('name'))
> ```

16. Joining Data Frames

```
        color  carcolor
name
John    Blue   NaN
George  Blue   Blue
Ringo   Purple NaN
```

It it easier to just use the .merge method.

The default join type for the .merge method is an *inner join*. The .merge method looks for common column names. It then aligns the values in those columns. If both data frames have values that are the same, they are kept along with the remaining columns from both data frames. Rows with values in the aligned columns that only appear in one data frame are discarded:

```
>>> df1.merge(df2)   # inner join
    color   name  carcolor
0   Blue    George  Blue
1   Purple  Ringo   NaN
```

When the how='outer' parameter setting is passed in, an *outer join* is performed. Again, the method looks for common column names. It aligns the values for those columns, and adds the values from the other columns of both data frames. If a either data frame had a value in the field that we join on that was absent from the other, the new columns are filled with NaN:

```
>>> df1.merge(df2, how='outer')
    color   name    carcolor
0   Blue    John    NaN
1   Blue    George  Blue
2   Purple  Ringo   NaN
3   NaN     Paul    Red
```

To perform a *left join*, pass the how='left' parameter setting. A left join keeps only the values from the overlapping columns in the data frame that the .merge method is called on. If the other data frame is missing aligned values, NaN is used to fill in their values:

```
>>> df1.merge(df2, how='left')
    color   name    carcolor
0   Blue    John    NaN
1   Blue    George  Blue
2   Purple  Ringo   NaN
```

Finally, there is support for a *right join* as well. A right join keeps the values from the overlapping columns in the data frame that is passed in as the first parameter of the .merge method. If the data frame that .merge was called on has aligned values, they are kept, otherwise NaN is used to fill in the missing values:

```
>>> df1.merge(df2, how='right')
```

```
     color    name carcolor
0     Blue  George     Blue
1   Purple   Ringo      NaN
2      NaN    Paul      Red
```

The .merge method has a few other parameters that turn out to be useful in practice. The table below lists them:

Parameter	Meaning
on	Column names to join on. String or list. (Default is intersection of names).
left_on	Column names for left data frame. String or list. Used when names don't overlap.
right_on	Column names for right data frame. String or list. Used when names don't overlap.
left_index	Join based on left data frame index. Boolean
right_index	Join based on right data frame index. Boolean

16.4 Summary

Data can often have more utility if we combine it with other data. In the 70's, *relational algebra* was invented to describe various joins among tabular data. The .merge method of the DataFrame lets us apply these operations to tabular data in the pandas world. This chapter described concatenation, and the four basic joins that are possible via .merge.

Chapter 17

Avalanche Analysis and Plotting

This chapter will walk through a data analysis and visualization project. It will also include many examples of plotting in pandas.

I live at the base of the Wasatch Mountains in Utah. In the winter it can snow quite a bit, which makes for great skiing. In order to get really great skiing (ie powder), you need to ski in a resort during a storm, be first in line at the resort the morning after a storm, or hike up a backcountry hill.

Hiking, or skinning up a hill, is quite a workout, but gives you access to fresh powder. In addition to wearing out your legs, one must also be cognizant of the threat of avalanches. It just so happens that aspects that make for great skiing also happen to be great avalanche paths. What follows is an analysis I did of the data collected by the Utah Avalanche Center[18].

17.1 Getting Data

The Utah Avalanche Center has great data, but lacks an API to get easy access to the data. I resorted to crawling the data, using the requests[19] and Beautiful Soup[20] libraries. By looking at the source of the data, we see that the table resides in a page that lists summaries of the avalanches, and another page that contains details.

From the HTML source of the overview page we find the following code:

---

[18]http://utahavalanchecenter.org/

[19]http://docs.python-requests.org/en/master/

[20]https://www.crummy.com/software/BeautifulSoup/

17. AVALANCHE ANALYSIS AND PLOTTING

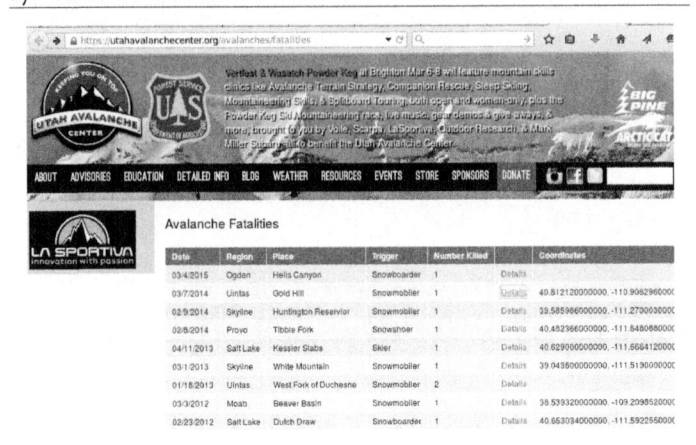

Figure 17.1: Figure showing overview of fatal avalanches

```
<div class="content">
  <div class="view view-avalanches view-id-avalanches
      view-display-id-page_1>
    <div class="view-content">
    <table class="views-table cols-7" >
      <thead>
      <tr>
        <th class="views-field
           views-field-field-occurrence-date" >Date</th>
        <th class="views-field
           views-field-field-region-forecaster" >Region</th>
        <th class="views-field
           views-field-field-region-forecaster-1" >Place</th>
        <th class="views-field
           views-field-field-trigger" >Trigger</th>
        <th class="views-field
           views-field-field-killed" >Number Killed</th>
        <th class="views-field
           views-field-view-node" ></th>
        <th class="views-field
           views-field-field-coordinates" >Coordinates</th>
      </tr>
      </thead>
      <tbody>
      <tr class="odd views-row-first">
        <td class="views-field
           views-field-field-occurrence-date" >
          <span class="date-display-single" property="dc:date"
              datatype="xsd:dateTime"
              content="2015-03-04T00:00:00-07:00">03/4/2015
          </span></td>
        <td class="views-field
           views-field-field-region-forecaster" >Ogden</td>
        <td class="views-field
```

160

17.1. Getting Data

```
        views-field-field-region-forecaster-1" >
          Hells Canyon</td>
      <td class="views-field
          views-field-field-trigger" >Snowboarder</td>
      <td class="views-field views-field-field-killed">1</td>
      <td class="views-field views-field-view-node" >
          <a href="/avalanches/23779">Details</a></td>
```

Upon inspection we see that inside of the <tr> elements are the names and values for data that might be interesting. We can pull the name off of the end of the class value that starts with views-field-field. The value is the text of the <td> element. For example, from the HTML below:

```
<td class="views-field
    views-field-field-region-forecaster" >Ogden</td>
```

There is a class attribute that has two space separated class names. The name is region-forecaster (the end of views-field-field-region-forecaster class name), and the value is Ogden.

Here is some code that will scrape this data:

```python
from bs4 import BeautifulSoup
import pandas as pd
import requests as r

base = 'https://utahavalanchecenter.org/'
url = base + 'avalanches/fatalities'

headers = {'User-Agent': 'Mozilla/5.0 (Macintosh; '\
    'Intel Mac OS X 10_10_1) AppleWebKit/537.36 (KHTML, '\
    'like Gecko) Chrome/39.0.2171.95 Safari/537.36'}


def get_avalanches(url):
    req = r.get(url, headers=headers)
    data = req.text

    soup = BeautifulSoup(data)
    content = soup.find(id="content")
    trs = content.find_all('tr')
    res = []
    for tr in trs:
        tds = tr.find_all('td')
        data = {}
        for td in tds:
            name, value = get_field_name_value(td)
            if not name:
                continue
            data[name] = value
        if data:
            res.append(data)
    return res
```

161

17. Avalanche Analysis and Plotting

```
def get_field_name_value(elem):
    tags = elem.get('class')
    start = 'views-field-field-'
    for t in tags:
        if t.startswith(start):
            return t[len(start):], ''.join(elem.stripped_strings)
        elif t == 'views-field-view-node':
            return 'url', elem.a['href']
    return None, None
```

The get_avalanches function spoofs a modern browser (see headers), and loops over all the table rows (<tr>) in the tag with an id set to content. It stores in a dictionary the names and values from the rows of information. The get_field_name_values takes in a <td> element and pulls out the names and values from it.

We can get a list of dictionaries per avalanche with the following line:

```
avs = get_avalanches(url)
```

At this point we have overview data. We want to crawl the detail page for each avalanche to get more information, such as elevation, slope, aspect, and more. The source of the detail page looks like this:

```
<div id="content" class="column"><div class="section">
  <a id="main-content"></a>
  <span class="title"><h1>Avalanche: East Kessler</h1></span>
  <div class="region region-content">
    <div id="block-system-main" class="block block-system">
      <div class="content">
        <div id="node-23838" class="node node-avalanche">
          <span property="dc:title"
                content="Avalanche: East Kessler">
            ...

          <div class="field field-name-field-observation-date
              field-type-datetime field-label-above">
            <div class="field-label">Observation Date</div>
            <div class="field-items">
              <div class="field-item even">
                Thursday, March 5, 2015
              </div>
            </div>
          </div>
```

The interesting data resides in <div> tags that have class set to field. The name is found in a <div> with class set to field-label and the value in a <div> with class set to field-item.

Here is some code that takes the base url and the dictionary containing the overview for that avalanche. It iterates over every class set to field and updates the dictionary with the detailed data:

```
def get_avalanche_detail(url, item):
```

17.1. Getting Data

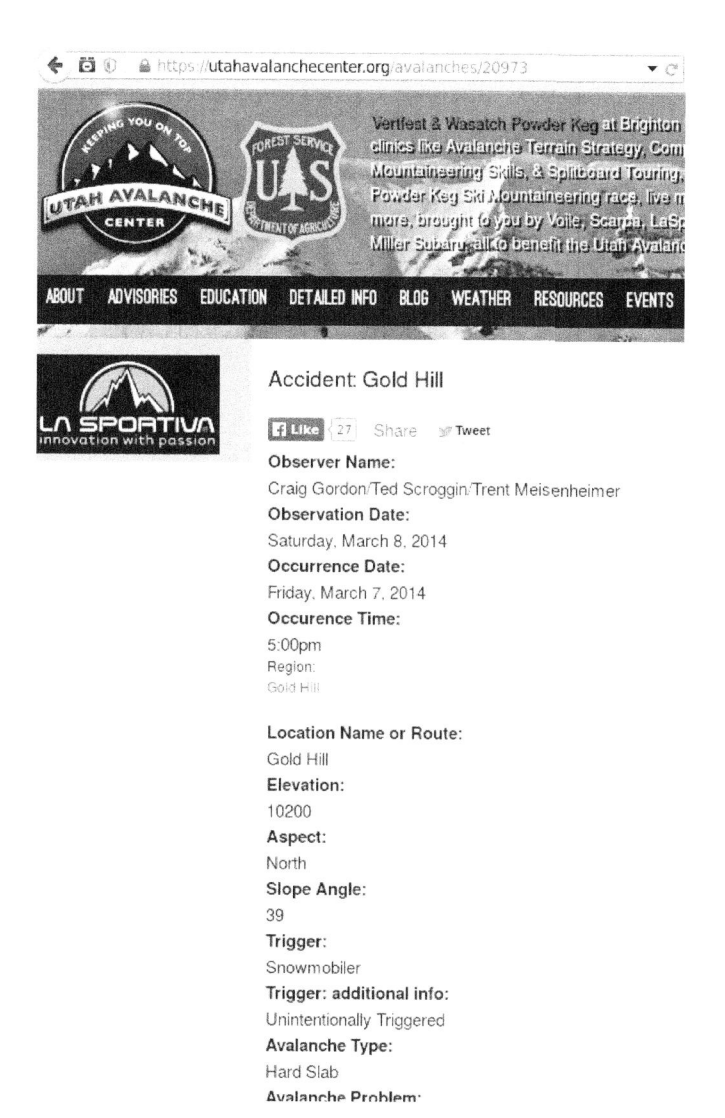

Figure 17.2: Figure showing details of fatal avalanches

17. Avalanche Analysis and Plotting

```
    req = r.get(url + item['url'], headers=headers)
    data = req.text

    soup = BeautifulSoup(data)
    content = soup.find(id='content')
    field_divs = content.find_all(class_='field')
    for div in field_divs:
        key_elem = div.find(class_='field-label')
        if key_elem is None:
            print("NONE!!!", div)
            continue
        key = ''.join(key_elem.stripped_strings)
        try:
            value_elem = div.find(class_='field-item')
            value = ''.join(value_elem.stripped_strings).\
                    replace(u'\xa0', u' ')
        except AttributeError as e:
            print(e, div)
        if key in item:
            continue
        item[key] = value
    return item

def get_avalanche_details(url, avs):
    res = []
    for item in avs:
        item = get_avalanche_detail(url, item)
        res.append(item)
    return res
```

With this code in hand we can create a data frame with the data by running the following code. Note that this takes about two minutes to scrape the data:

```
details = get_avalanche_details(base, avs)
df = pd.DataFrame(details)
```

Sometimes you can get your data by querying a database or using an API. Sometimes you need to resort to scraping.

17.2 Munging Data

At this point we have the data, now we want to inspect it, clean it, and munge it. In other words, we get to be a data janitor.

If you want to try this on your computer, you can get access to the scraped data[21] on my GitHub account.

The first thing to do is to check out the datatypes of the columns. We want to make sure we have numeric data, and datetime data in addition to strings:

---

[21]https://github.com/mattharrison/UtahAvalanche/blob/master/ava-all.csv

17.2. Munging Data

```
>>> df = pd.read_csv('data/ava-all.csv')
>>> df.dtypes
Unnamed: 0                              int64
Accident and Rescue Summary:            object
Aspect:                                 object
Avalanche Problem:                      object
Avalanche Type:                         object
Buried - Fully:                         float64
Buried - Partly:                        float64
Carried:                                float64
Caught:                                 float64
Comments:                               object
Coordinates:                            object
Depth:                                  object
Elevation:                              object
Injured:                                float64
Killed:                                 int64
Location Name or Route:                 object
Observation Date:                       object
Observer Name:                          object
Occurence Time:                         object
Occurrence Date:                        object
Region:                                 object
Slope Angle:                            float64
Snow Profile Comments:                  object
Terrain Summary:                        object
Trigger:                                object
Trigger: additional info:               object
Vertical:                               object
Video:                                  float64
Weak Layer:                             object
Weather Conditions and History:         object
Width:                                  object
coordinates                             object
killed                                  int64
occurrence-date                         object
region-forecaster                       object
region-forecaster-1                     object
trigger                                 object
url                                     object
dtype: object
```

It looks like some of the values are numeric, though the type of Occurrence Date is object, which means it is a string and not a datetime object. We will address that later.

165

17. Avalanche Analysis and Plotting

Note

Because I read this data from the CSV file, pandas tried its hardest to coerce numeric values. Had I simply converted the list of dictionaries from the crawled data, the type for all of the columns would have been object, the string data type (because the scraping returned strings).

17.3 Describing Data

Now, let's inspect the data and see what it looks like. First let's look at the shape:

```
>>> df.shape
(92, 38)
```

This tells us there were 92 rows and 38 columns.

Let'd dig in a little deeper with some summary statistics. A simple way to do this is with .describe:

```
>>> print(df.describe().to_string(line_width=60))
       Unnamed: 0  Buried - Fully:  Buried - Partly:  \
count   92.00000        64.000000         22.000000
mean    45.50000         1.156250          1.090909
std     26.70206         0.365963          0.294245
min      0.00000         1.000000          1.000000
25%     22.75000         1.000000          1.000000
50%     45.50000         1.000000          1.000000
75%     68.25000         1.000000          1.000000
max     91.00000         2.000000          2.000000

          Carried:     Caught:  Injured:    Killed:  \
count    71.000000   72.000000       5.0  92.000000
mean      1.591549    1.638889       1.0   1.163043
std       1.049863    1.091653       0.0   0.475260
min       1.000000    1.000000       1.0   1.000000
25%       1.000000    1.000000       1.0   1.000000
50%       1.000000    1.000000       1.0   1.000000
75%       2.000000    2.000000       1.0   1.000000
max       7.000000    7.000000       1.0   4.000000

       Slope Angle:  Video:     killed
count     42.000000     0.0  92.000000
mean      37.785714     NaN   1.163043
std        5.567921     NaN   0.475260
min       10.000000     NaN   1.000000
25%       36.000000     NaN   1.000000
50%       38.000000     NaN   1.000000
75%       40.000000     NaN   1.000000
max       50.000000     NaN   4.000000
```

There are a few takeaways from this. Unamed: 0 is the index column that was serialized to CSV. We will ignore that column.

17.3. Describing Data

`Buried - Fully:` is a column that counts how many people were completely buried in the avalanche. It looks like 64 avalanches had people that were buried. The average number of people buried was 1.15, the minimum was 1 and the maximum was 2. The fact that the minimum and maximum numbers are whole is probably good. It wouldn't make sense that 3.5 people was the maximum.

Another thing to note is that although the minimum was 1.0, there were only 64 avalanches that had entries. That means the remaining avalanches had no entries (NaN). This is probably wrong, though it is hard to tell. NaN could mean that the reporters did not know whether there were buries. Another option is that it means that there were zero buries. Though I suspect the later with recent avalanches, it could be the former with older entries.

I will leave that data, but we can see if we interpret NaN to really mean 0, then it tells a different story, as the average number of buries drops to .8:

```
>>> df['Buried - Fully:'].fillna(0).describe()
count    92.000000
mean      0.804348
std       0.615534
min       0.000000
25%       0.000000
50%       1.000000
75%       1.000000
max       2.000000
Name: Buried - Fully:, dtype: float64
```

We could do this for each of the numeric columns here and decide whether we need to change them. If we had access to the someone who knows the data a little better, we could ask them how to resolve such issues.

On an aesthetic note, there are a bunch of columns with colons on the end. Let's clean that up, by replacing colons with an empty string:

```
>>> df = df.rename(columns={x:x.replace(':', '')
...     for x in df.columns})
```

Note

The above uses a *dictionary comprehension* to create a dictionary from the columns. The syntax:

```
new_cols = {x:x.replace(':', '') for x in df2.columns}
```

Is the same as:

17. Avalanche Analysis and Plotting

```
new_cols = {}
for x in df2.columns:
    new_cols[x] = x.replace(':', '')
```

17.4 Categorical Data

The columns that don't appear in the output of .describe are columns that have non-numeric values. Let's inspect a few of them. Many of them are *categorical*, in that they don't have free form text, but only a limited set of options. A nice way to inspect a categorical column is to view the results of the .value_counts column.

Let's inspect the "Aspect" column. In avalanche terms, the aspect is the direction that the slope faces:

```
>>> df.Aspect.value_counts()
Northeast    24
North        14
East          9
Northwest     9
West          3
Southeast     3
South         1
Name: Aspect, dtype: int64
```

This tells us that slopes that are facing north-east are more prone to slide. Or does it? Skiers tend to ski the north and east aspects. Because they stay out of the sun, the snow stays softer. One should be careful to draw the conclusion that skiing south-facing aspects will prevent one from finding themselves in an avalanche. It is probably the opposite, as the freeze-thaw cycles from the sun can cause instability that leads to slides. (It also happens to be the case that the snow is generally worse to ski on).

Let's look at another categorical column, the "Avalanche Type":

```
>>> df["Avalanche Type"].value_counts()
Hard Slab       27
Soft Slab       24
Wet Slab         1
Cornice Fall     1
Name: Avalanche Type, dtype: int64
```

This column indicates the type of avalanche. By summing these values we can see that many are empty:

```
>>> df["Avalanche Type"].value_counts().sum()
53
```

Again, the lack of data could indicate an unknown type of avalanche, or that the reporter forgot to note this. As almost 40% of the incidents are missing values, it might be hard to infer too much from this. Perhaps the missing 40% were all "Cornice Fall"? Were they not really avalanches? Is just the older data missing classifications? (Perhaps the methodology has changed over time). These are the sorts of questions that need answering when you start digging into data.

17.5 Converting Column Types

One value that should be numeric, but didn't show up in .describe is the "Depth" column. This column reports on the depth of snowpack that slid during the avalanche. Let's look a little deeper:

```
>>> df.Depth.head(15)
0        3'
1        4'
2        4'
3       18"
4        8"
5        2'
6        3'
7        2'
8       16"
9        3'
10     2.5'
11      16"
12      NaN
13     3.5'
14       8'
Name: Depth, dtype: object
```

Here we can see that this field is free-form. Free-form text is a data janitors nightmare. Sometimes, it was entered as inches, other times as feet, and occasionally it was missing. As is, it hard to quantify. There is no out-of-the-box functionality for converting text like this to numbers in pandas, so we will not be able to take advantage of vectorized built-ins. But we can pull out a sledgehammer from the python standard library to help us, the regular expression.

Here is a function that takes a string as input and tries to coerce it to a number of inches:

```
>>> import re
>>> def to_inches(orig):
...     txt = str(orig)
...     if txt == 'nan':
...         return orig
...     reg = r'''(((\d*\.)?\d*)')?(((\d*\.)?\d*)")?'''
...     mo = re.search(reg, txt)
...     feet = mo.group(2) or 0
...     inches = mo.group(5) or 0
...     return float(feet) * 12 + float(inches)
```

169

17. Avalanche Analysis and Plotting

The to_inches function returns NaN if that comes in as the orig parameter. Otherwise, it looks for optional feet (numbers followed by a single quote) and optional inches (numbers followed by a double quote). It casts these to floating point numbers and multiplies the feet by twelve. Finally, it returns the sum.

Note

Regular expressions could fill up a book on their own. A few things to note. We use *raw strings* to specifiy them (they have an r at the front), as raw strings don't interpret backslash as an escape character. This is important because the backslash has special meaning in regular expressions. \d means match a digit.

The parentheses are used to specify groups. After invoking the search function, we get *match objects* as results (mo in the code above). The .group method pulls out the match inside of the group. mo.group(2) looks for the second left parenthesis and returns the match inside of those parentheses. mo.group(5) looks for the fifth left parentheses, and the match inside of it. Normally Python is zero-based, where we start counting from zero, but in the case of regular expression groups, we start counting at one. The first left parenthesis indicates where the first group starts, group one, not zero.

Let's add a new column to store the depth of the avalanche in inches:

```
>>> df['depth_inches'] = df.Depth.apply(to_inches)
```

Now, let's inspect it to make sure it looks ok:

```
>>> df.depth_inches.describe()
count    61.000000
mean     32.573770
std      17.628064
min       0.000000
25%      24.000000
50%      30.000000
75%      42.000000
max      96.000000
Name: depth_inches, dtype: float64
```

Note that we are still missing values here, which is a little troubling because an avalanche by definition is snow sliding down a hill, and if no snow slid down, how do you have an avalanche? If you wanted to assume that the median is a good default value you could use the following:

```
df['depth_inches'] = df.depth_inches.fiillna(
    df.depth_inches.median)
```

170

17.6. Dealing with Dates

Another column that should be numeric is the "Vertical" column. This indicates how many vertical feet the avalanche slid. We can see the that dtype is object:

```
>>> df.Vertical.head(15)
0         1500
1          200
2          175
3          125
4         1500
5          250
6           50
7         1000
8          600
9          350
10        2500
11         800
12         900
13       Unknown
14        1000
Name: Vertical, dtype: object
```

pandas probably would have coerced this to a numeric column if that pesky "Unknown" wasn't in there. Is that really different than NaN? Using the to_numeric function, we can force this column to be numeric. If we pass errors='coerce', then "Unknown" will be converted to NaN:

```
>>> df['vert'] = pd.to_numeric(df.Vertical,
...      errors='coerce')
```

17.6 Dealing with Dates

Let's look at the "Occurrence Date" column:

```
>>> df['Occurrence Date'].head()
0      Wednesday, March 4, 2015
1         Friday, March 7, 2014
2       Sunday, February 9, 2014
3      Saturday, February 8, 2014
4       Thursday, April 11, 2013
Name: Occurrence Date, dtype: object
```

Note that the dtype is object, so as is, we cannot perform date analysis on this. In this case, pandas does have a function for coercion, the to_datetime function:

```
>>> pd.to_datetime(df['Occurrence Date']).head()
0    2015-03-04
1    2014-03-07
2    2014-02-09
3    2014-02-08
4    2013-04-11
```

17. AVALANCHE ANALYSIS AND PLOTTING

```
Name: Occurrence Date, dtype: datetime64[ns]
```

That's better, the dtype is datetime64[ns] for this. Let's make a column for year, so we can see yearly trends. Date columns in pandas have a .dt attribute, that allows us to pull date parts out of it:

```
>>> df['year'] = pd.to_datetime(
...     df['Occurrence Date']).dt.year
```

The following table lists the attributes found on the .dt attribute:

Attribute	Result
date	Date without timestamp
day	Day of month
dayofweek	Day number (Monday=0)
dayofyear	Day of year
days_in_month	Number of days in month
daysinmonth	Number of days in month
hour	Hours of timestamp
is_month_end	Is last day of month
is_month_start	Is first day of month
is_quarter_end	Is last day of quarter
is_quarter_start	Is first day of quarter
is_year_end	Is last day of year
is_year_start	Is first day of year
microsecond	Microseconds of timestamp
minute	Minutes of timestamp
month	Month number (Jan=1)
nanosecond	Nanoseconds of timestamp
quarter	Quarter of date
second	Seconds of timestamp
time	Time without date
tz	Timezone
week	Week of year
weekday	Day number (Monday=0)
weekofyear	Week of year
year	Year

Let's look at what day of the week avalanches occur on. The dt attribute has the weekday and dayofweek attribute (both are the same):

```
>>> dates = pd.to_datetime(df['Occurrence Date'])
>>> dates.dt.dayofweek.value_counts()
5    29
6    14
4    14
2    10
0    10
```

17.7. Splitting a Column into Two Columns

```
3       9
1       6
Name: Occurrence Date, dtype: int64
```

This gives us the number of the weekday. We could use the `.replace` method to map the integer to the string value of the weekday. In this case, we can see that every date in the original "Occurrence Date" has the day of week and there are no missing values:

```
>>> df['Occurrence Date'].isnull().any()
False
```

Another option to get the weekday name is to split it off of the string:

```
>>> df['dow'] = df['Occurrence Date'].apply(
...     lambda x: x.split(',')[0])

>>> df.dow.value_counts()
Saturday    29
Sunday      14
Friday      14
Monday      10
Wednesday   10
Thursday     9
Tuesday      6
Name: dow, dtype: int64
```

Apparently skiing on Tuesday is the safest day. Again, this is a silly conclusion as the day doesn't determine whether a slide will occur. You need to have insight into your data in order to draw conclusions from it.

17.7 Splitting a Column into Two Columns

Another problematic column is the "coordinates" column:

```
>>> df.coordinates.head()
0                                      NaN
1    40.812120000000, -110.906296000000
2    39.585986000000, -111.270003000000
3    40.482366000000, -111.648088000000
4    40.629000000000, -111.666412000000
Name: coordinates, dtype: object
```

This column has both the latitude and longitude embedded in it in string form. Or, it might be empty. We will need some logic to pull these values out. Here we use a function to tease the latitude out:

```
>>> def lat(val):
...     if str(val) == 'nan':
```

17. Avalanche Analysis and Plotting

```
...                 return val
...         else:
...                 return float(val.split(',')[0])
>>> df['lat'] = df.coordinates.apply(lat)
```

We can describe the result to see if it worked. The values should be centered pretty evenly, because these are located in Utah:

```
>>> df.lat.describe()
count    78.000000
mean     39.483177
std       6.472255
min       0.000000
25%      40.415395
50%      40.602058
75%      40.668936
max      41.711752
Name: lat, dtype: float64
```

In this case, we see there is a minimum of 0. This is bad data. A latitude of zero is not in Utah. We will to address that in a bit. First let's address longitude. This time we will use a lambda function. This function does almost the same thing as our lat function above, except it uses an index of 1. I don't consider this code very readable, but wanted to show that a lambda function could be used to perform this logic:

```
>>> df['lon'] = df.coordinates.apply(
...     lambda x: float(x.split(',')[1]) if str(x) != 'nan' \
...     else x)
```

Again, we can do a quick sanity check with .describe:

```
>>> df.lon.describe()
count     78.000000
mean    -108.683679
std       17.748443
min     -111.969482
25%     -111.679808
50%     -111.611396
75%     -111.517262
max        0.000000
Name: lon, dtype: float64
```

We still have the zero value problem. On the longitude we see 0 in the max location, because the values are negative. Let's address these zeros:

```
>>> df['lat'] = df.lat.replace(0, float('nan'))
>>> df['lon'] = df.lon.replace(0, float('nan'))
>>> df.lon.describe()
count     76.000000
mean    -111.543775
std        0.357423
```

```
min      -111.969482
25%      -111.683284
50%      -111.614593
75%      -111.520059
max      -109.209852
Name: lon, dtype: float64
```

Much better! No zeros. Though, this means that we cannot plot these avalanches on our map. If we were eager enough, we could probably determine these coordinates by hand, by reading the description. Averaging out the latitudes, and longitudes of the other slides would probably not be effective here to fill in these missing values.

17.8 Analysis

The final product of my analysis was an infographic containing various chunks of information derived from the data. The first part was the number of fatal avalanches since 1995[22]:

```
>>> ava95 = df[df.year >= 1995]
>>> len(ava95)
61
```

I also calculated the total number of casualties. This is just the sum of the "killed" column:

```
>>> ava95.killed.sum()
72
```

The next part of my infographic was a plot of count of people killed vs year. Here's some code to plot that information:

```
>>> ax = fig.add_subplot(111)
>>> ava95.groupby('year').sum().reset_index(
...      ).plot.scatter(x='year', y='killed', ax=ax)
>>> fig.savefig('/tmp/pd-ava-1.png')
```

In the table below we summarize the various plot types that pandas supports for data frames.

---

[22]The folks at the Utah Avalanche Center approached me after I released my infographic and ask that I redo the data with only details from 1995, as they claimed that the data from prior years was less reliable.

17. AVALANCHE ANALYSIS AND PLOTTING

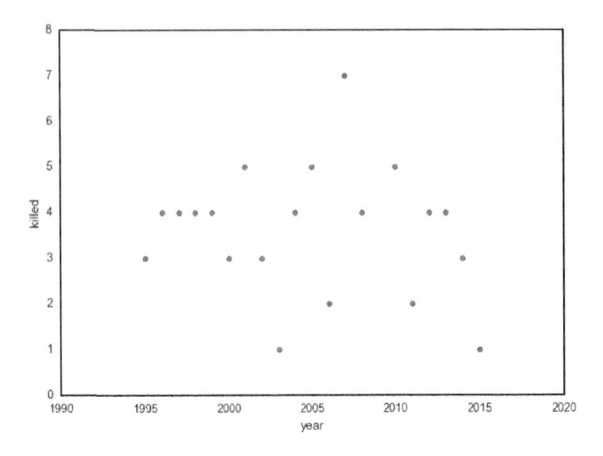

Figure 17.3: A figure illustrating plotting deaths over time

plot *Methods*	*Result*
plot.area	Creates an area plot for numeric columns
plot.bar	Creates a bar plot for numeric columns
plot.barh	Creates a horizontal bar plot for numeric columns
plot.box	Creates a box plot for numeric columns
plot.density	Creates a kernel density estimation plot for numeric columns (also plot.kde)
plot.hexbin	Creates a hexbin plot. Requires x and y parameters
plot.hist	Creates a histogram for numeric columns
plot.line	Create a line plot. Plots index on x column, and numeric column values for y
plot.pie	Create a pie plot. Requires y parameter or subplots=True for DataFrame
plot.scatter	Create a scatter plot. Requires x and y parameters

The code to plot is a mouthful. Let's examine what is going on. First we groupby the "year" column. We sum all of the numeric columns. The result of this is a data frame with the index containing the years and the columns being the sum of the numeric columns. We call .reset_index on this to push the index of years that we just grouped by back into a column. On this data frame we call .plot.scatter and pass in the x and y columns we want to use. (We reset the index so we could pass 'year' to x).

In my infographic, I ended up using the Seaborn[23] library, because it has a regplot function that will insert a regression line for us. I also changed the marker to an X, and passed in a dictionary

17.9. Plotting on Maps

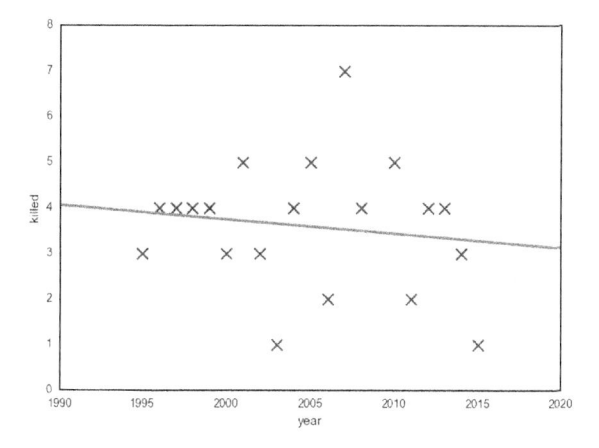

Figure 17.4: A figure illustrating plotting deaths over time, with a regression line compliments of the seaborn library. Note that Seaborn changes the default aesthetics of matplotlib.

to scatter_kws to make the size larger and set the color to a shade of red:

```
>>> import seaborn as sns
>>> ax = fig.add_subplot(111)
>>> summed = ava95.groupby('year').sum().reset_index()
>>> sns.regplot(x='year', y='killed', data=summed,
...     lowess=0, marker='x',
...     scatter_kws={'s':100, 'color':'#a40000'})
>>> fig.savefig('/tmp/pd-ava-2.png')
```

Rather than saving this as a png file, I saved it as an SVG file. This gave me the ability to edit the graph in a vector editor and the final product ended up slightly tweaked.

17.9 Plotting on Maps

Matplotlib has the ability to plot on maps, but to be honest it is painful, and the result is static. A better option if you are using Jupyter notebooks for analysis is to use Folium[24]. Folium provides

---
[23]https://stanford.edu/~mwaskom/software/seaborn/

17. Avalanche Analysis and Plotting

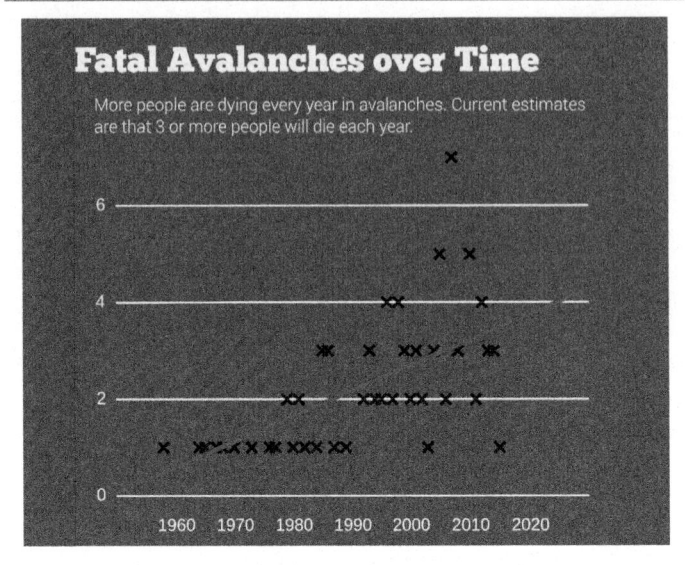

Fatal Avalanches over Time

More people are dying every year in avalanches. Current estimates are that 3 or more people will die each year.

Figure 17.5: A figure illustrating avalanche deaths in Utah, since 1960. This was created with Python, pandas, and Seaborn. Later the image was imported into Inkscape to add text and tweak. In this book, we examine deaths since 1995.

an interactive map very similar to Google Maps, which is useable inside of Jupyter.

After a quick `pip install folium` and running the following code in Jupyter, you will have a nice little map. The code puts markers at the latitude and longitude of the slide event, and it also embeds the "Accident and Rescue Summary" column in a popup:

```
import folium
from IPython.display import HTML

def inline_map(map):
    map._build_map()
    return HTML('''<iframe srcdoc="{srcdoc}"
    style="width: 100%; height: 500px;">
    </iframe>
    '''.format(srcdoc=map.HTML.replace('"', '&quot;')))
def summary(i, row):
    return '''<b>{} {} {} {}</b>
    <p>{}</p>
    '''.format(i, row['year'], row['Trigger'],
```

[24] https://folium.readthedocs.org/en/latest/

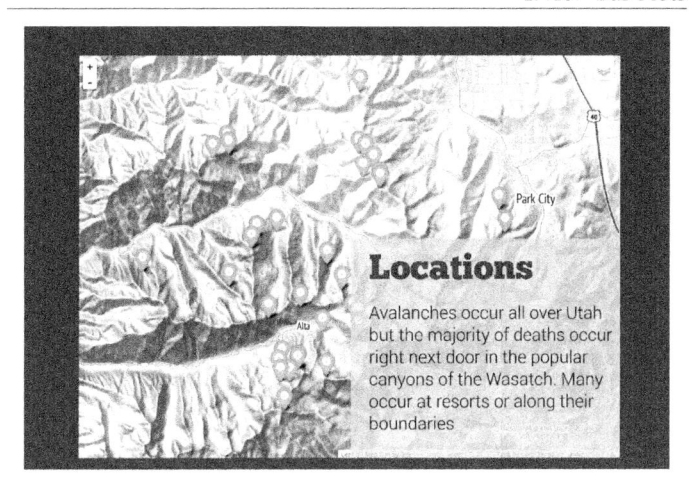

Figure 17.6: A figure illustrating a portion of the Folium map used in the infographic.

```
                row['Location Name or Route'],
                row['Accident and Rescue Summary'])
center = [40.5, -111.5]
map = folium.Map(location=center, zoom_start=10,
                tiles='Stamen Terrain', height=700)
for i, row in ava95.iterrows():
    if str(row.lat) == 'nan':
        continue
    map.simple_marker([row.lat, row.lon], popup=summary(r, row))

inline_map(map)
```

An image of the map was added to the infographic with some explanatory text.

17.10 Bar Plots

I included a few bar plots, because they allow for quick comparisons. I wanted to show what triggered slides, and at which elevations they occur. This is simple in pandas.

Because the "Trigger" column is categorical, we can use the .value_counts method to view distribution:

```
>>> ava95.Trigger.value_counts()
Snowmobiler    25
Skier          14
Snowboarder    12
Unknown         3
```

17. AVALANCHE ANALYSIS AND PLOTTING

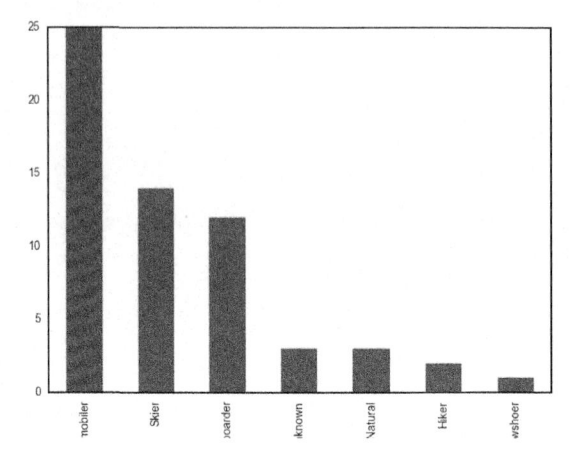

Figure 17.7: Figure illustrating triggers of avalanches.

```
Natural      3
Hiker        2
Snowshoer    1
Name: Trigger, dtype: int64
```

To make this into a bar plot, simply add .plot.bar():

```
>>> ax = fig.add_subplot(111)
>>> ava95.Trigger.value_counts().plot.bar(ax=ax)
>>> fig.savefig('/tmp/pd-ava-3.png')
```

For the infographic, I added a few graphics, and text to spice it up.

I also wanted a visualization of the elevations at which avalanches occur. I used a horizontal histogram plot for this, so I called .plot.hist(orientation='horizontal'). Sadly, the column data type was set to string as it contained Unknown in it. In order to get a histogram we need to convert it to a numeric column. Not a problem, we just need to wrap the column with pd.to_numeric:

```
>>> ax = fig.add_subplot(111)
>>> pd.to_numeric(ava95.Elevation, errors='coerce')\
...     .plot.hist(orientation='horizontal', ax=ax)
>>> fig.savefig('/tmp/pd-ava-4.png')
```

17.10. Bar Plots

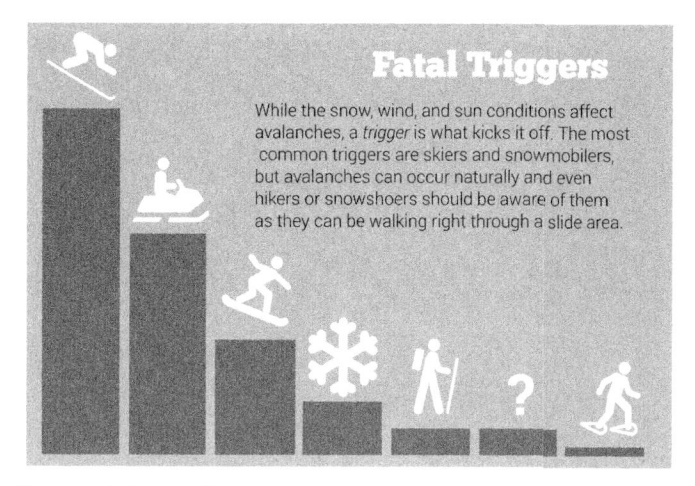

Figure 17.8: Figure illustrating triggers of avalanches used in infographic.

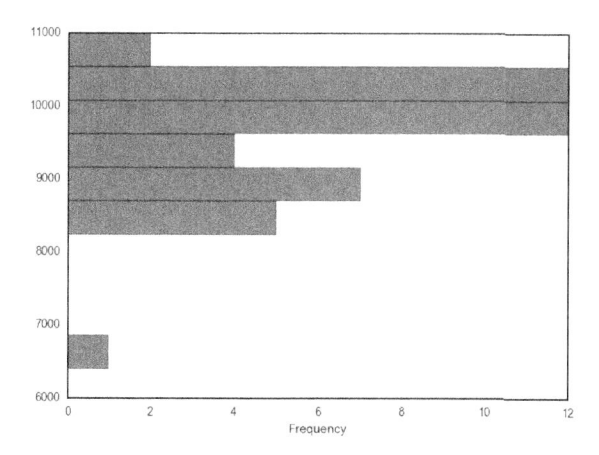

Figure 17.9: Figure illustrating horizontal histogram of avalanche elevations.

181

17. Avalanche Analysis and Plotting

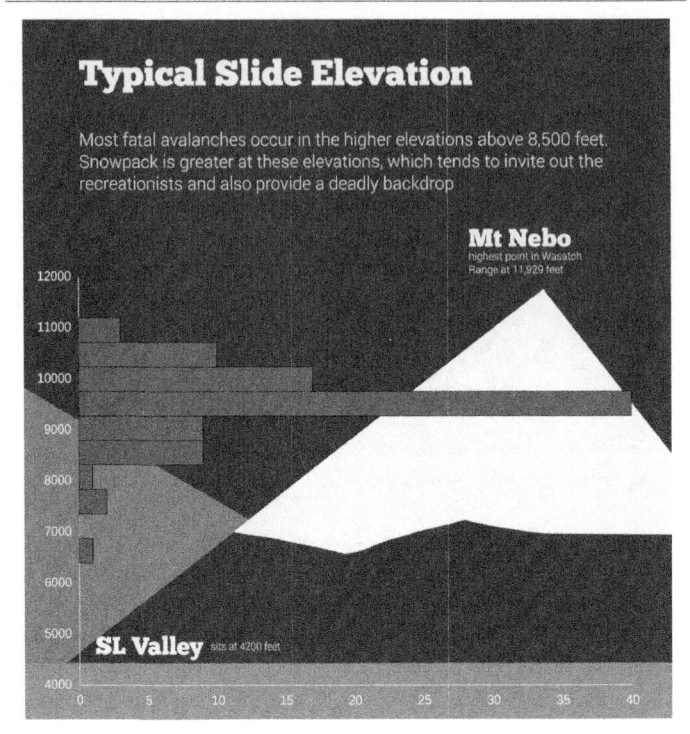

[Typical Slide Elevation infographic]

Figure 17.10: Figure illustrating plot of avalanche elevations used in infographic. The plot is slightly different, as this had older data. I also added in the highest peak and the valley floor to give some sense of scale.

17.11 Assorted Plots

Infographics with images are better, so I had a few more images related to avalanches. One was a graph of the slopes where the snow slid. I added a little jitter to the slopes and changed the alpha values so they show up better:

```
>>> import math
>>> import random

>>> def to_rad(d):
...     return d* math.pi / 180

>>> ax = plt.subplot(111)
>>> for i, row in df.iterrows():
...     jitter = (random.random() - .5)*.2
```

17.11. Assorted Plots

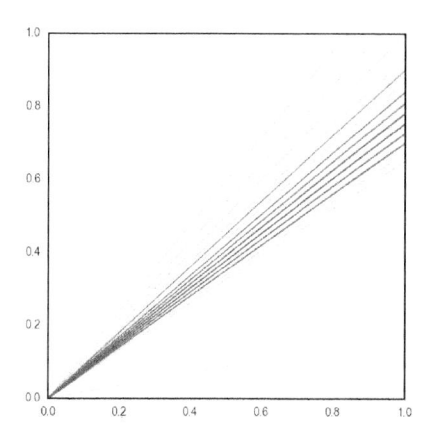

Figure 17.11: Figure illustrating plot of avalanche slopes. Note that the default ratio of the plot is not square, hence the call to ax.set_aspect('equal', adjustable='box').

```
...         plt.plot([0, 1], [0, math.tan(to_rad(row['Slope Angle'] +
...             jitter))], alpha=.3, color='b', linewidth=1)
>>> ax.set_xlim(0, 1)
>>> ax.set_ylim(0, 1)
>>> ax.set_aspect('equal', adjustable='box')
>>> fig.savefig('/tmp/pd-ava-5.png')
```

For the infographic version, I added some text explaining the outlier in my SVG editor, and a protractor to help visualize the angles.

Another image that I included was a rose plot of the aspects. The matplotlib library has the ability to plot in polar coordinates, so I converted the categorical values of the "Aspect" column into degrees and plotted that:

```
>>> mapping = {'North': 90, 'Northeast': 45, 'East': 0,
...     'Southeast': 315, 'South': 270, 'Southwest':225,
...     'West': 180, 'Northwest': 135}
>>> ax = plt.subplot(111, projection='polar')
>>> s = df.Aspect.value_counts()
>>> items = list(s.items())
>>> thetas = [to_rad(mapping[x[0]]-22.5) for x in items]
>>> radii = [x[1] for x in items]
>>> bars = ax.bar(thetas, radii)
>>> fig.savefig('/tmp/pd-ava-6.png')
```

17. Avalanche Analysis and Plotting

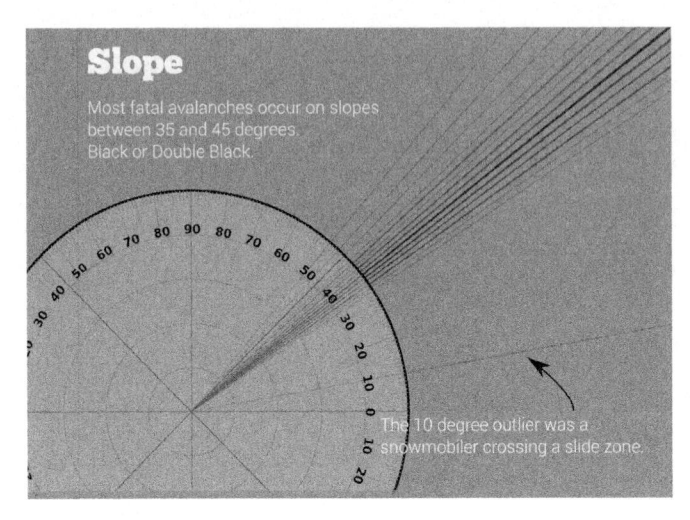

Figure 17.12: Figure illustrating slopes in the infographic

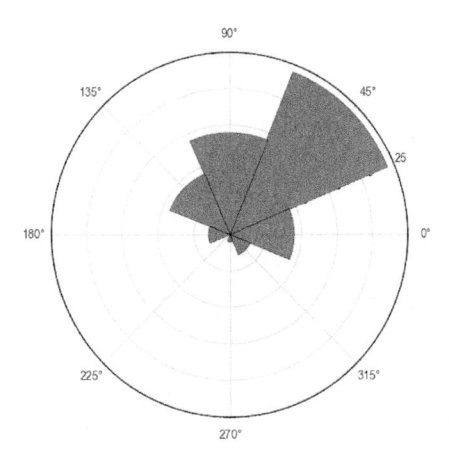

Figure 17.13: Figure illustrating ratios of avalanche aspects.

17.12. Summary

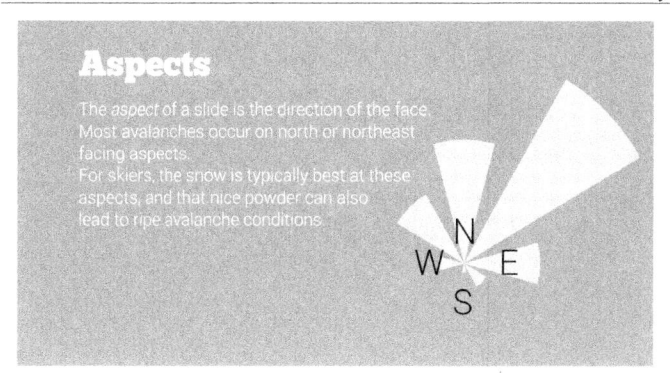

Figure 17.14: Figure illustrating aspects in the infographic.

The final image in the infographic was touched up slightly in the vector editor, but you can see that matplotlib is responsible for the graphic portion.

17.12 Summary

In this chapter we looked at a sample project. Even without a database or CSV file floating around, we were able to scrape the data from a website. Then, using pandas, we did some pretty heavy janitorial work on the data. Finally, we were able to do some analysis and generate some plots of the data. Since matplotlib has the ability to save as SVG, we were able to import these plots into a vector editor, and create a fancy infographic from them.

This should give you a feel for the kind of work that pandas will enable. Combined with the power of Python, you are only limited by your imagination. (And your free time).

Chapter 18

Summary

Thanks for learning about the pandas library. Hopefully, as you have read through this book, you have begun to appreciate the power in this library. You might be wondering what to do now that you have finished this book?

I've taught many people Python and pandas over the years, and they typically question what to do to continue learning. My answer is pretty simple: find a project that you would like to work on and find an excuse to use Python or pandas. If you are in a business setting and use Excel, try to see if you can replicate what you do in Jupyter and pandas. If you are interested in Machine Learning, check out Kaggle for projects to try out your new skills. Or simply find some data about something you are interested in and start playing around.

For those who like videos and screencasts, I offer a screencast service called PyCast[25] which has many examples of using Python and pandas in various projects.

As pandas is an open source project, you can contribute and improve the library. The library is still in active development.

---

[25] https://pycast.io

About the Author

Matt Harrison has been using Python since 2000. He runs MetaSnake, a Python and Data Science consultancy and corporate training shop. In the past, he has worked across the domains of search, build management and testing, business intelligence and storage.

He has presented and taught tutorials at conferences such as Strata, SciPy, SCALE, PyCON and OSCON as well as local user conferences. The structure and content of this book is based off of first hand experience teaching Python to many individuals.

He blogs at hairysun.com and occasionally tweets useful Python related information at @__mharrison__.

Index

!=, 37
*, 37
+, 37, 109
-, 37
..., 12
/, 37
//, 37
<, 37
==, 37
>, 37
>>>, 12
%, 37
&, 33, 37, 147
__contains__, 21, 107
__iter__, 21, 106
^, 37
~, 33

agg(func), 133
all, 125, 133, 148
anaconda, 5
any, 125, 146
append, 23, 56, 98
apply, 60, 148
apply(func), 133
apt-get, 6
as_matrix, 112
astype, 52
at, 29
attribute access, 39
autocorr, 51
axes, 105
axes, 89
axis, 103

axis, 89
axis=1, 117, 154

bar plot, 68
Beautiful Soup, 161
bfill, 149
boolean array, 16, 31
boolean operations, 33
broadcasting, 31, 109

cat, 64
categorical data, 168
center, 64
clip, 52, 127
closed interval, 120
coerce, 52
column joining, 156
columns, 105
concat, 98, 153
concatenating columns, 154
concatenating rows, 153
conda, 5
contains, 64
convert_objects, 52
copy, 35
corr, 50, 94, 128
corrwith, 128
count, 46, 64, 125, 133
cov, 50
cumprod, 51
cumsum, 51

data structures, 9
DataFrame, 86
DataFrame, 9

191

Index

date conversion, 171
decode, 64
del, 23
delete column, 102
describe, 48, 94, 124
destructuring, 36
dictionary comprehension, 167
diff, 51
dimension, 136
dot, 55, 110
drop, 101, 103, 116
drop column, 102
drop_duplicates, 46
dropna, 53, 147
dt, 172
dtype, 52, 108
dummy variable, 140
duplicate index, 22, 47
duplicate values, 46
duplicated, 46

encode, 64
endswith, 64
Excel, 112
ExcelWriter, 112

fact, 136
ffill, 149
fillna, 38, 53, 148
findall, 64
first_valid_index, 55
for, 21
from_csv, 62, 78
from_dict, 111

get, 39, 40, 64
get_dummies, 140
get_value, 39, 40, 114
getting values in a data frame, 114
getvalue, 111
groupby, 131
groupby (series), 47

half-open interval, 120
head, 118
hist, 49, 69

iat, 29, 114
idmin, 48
idxmax, 48, 130, 133
idxmin, 130, 133
ignore_index, 100
iloc, 22, 27, 86, 118
in, 21
in (data frame), 107
in-place, 57
index, 44, 101, 105
index, 12, 13, 25
index joining, 155
indicator variable, 140
info, 106
inner join, 155, 156
inplace, 35
insert, 115
inserting columns, 115
inserting missing data, 148
interpolate, 149
is_unique, 25
isnull, 54, 146
iteration, 36
iteration (data frame), 106
iteration, series, 21
iteritems, 21, 36, 107
iterrows, 108
itertuples, 108
ix, 30

join, 64, 155
joins, 155

Kendall Correlation, 128
kernel density estimation, 69
keys, 107
keywords, 42
kurt, 50, 129

label based indexing, 28
last, 133
last_valid_index, 55
left join, 155, 156
len, 64, 109
line plot, 67
loc, 28
long data, 136

192

Index

lower, 64
lstrip, 64

mad, 49, 129
map, 59
mask, 31
match, 64
matplotlib, 67
matrix operations, 110
max, 48, 133
mean, 47, 129, 133
median, 47, 133
melt, 136
membership, series, 21
merge, 156
min, 48, 133
missing data, 148

namedtuple, 108
NaN, 15, 53
notnull, 54, 147
nth, 133
NumPy, 16, 88, 112
nunique, 46

OLAP, 136
orient, 111
outer join, 155, 156

pad, 64
Panel, 9
Pearson Correlation, 94, 128
pip, 6
pivot table, 131
pivot_table, 134
plot, 67, 71, 95, 175
plot(kind='kde'), 69
plotting, 67
pop, 102, 116
position based indexing, 27
precedence, 33
prod, 129, 133

quantile, 47, 133

rank, 59, 126
read_csv, 63, 88, 105

read_excel, 112
read_table, 145
regex, 116
regular expression, 116
regular expressions, 169
reindex, 43, 113, 116
remove column, 103
rename, 44
repeat, 57, 64
replace, 64, 115, 116, 150
Requests, 161
reserved words, 41
reset_index, 43
right join, 155, 156
right_ax, 95
rstrip, 64

savefig, 67
scalar, 20
secondary_y, 95
sem, 133
Series, 12, 19
Series, 9
set_index, 113
set_value, 39, 42, 114
set_ylabel, 95
setting values in a data frame, 114
shape, 106
size, 133
skew, 49, 129
slice, 64
slice, 28
slicing, 31, 118
sort, 57
sort_index, 59, 122
sort_values, 121
sorting data frames, 121
Spearman Correlation, 128
split, 64
stable sort, 58
stack, 141
startswith, 64
std, 49, 133
str, 63
str.findall, 63
str.lower, 63

193

INDEX

stride, 31
strip, 64
sum, 47, 128, 133

T, 55, 110
tail, 118
tidy data, 139
title, 64
to_csv, 61, 111
to_datetime, 52, 171
to_dict, 111
to_excel, 112
to_numeric, 52, 171
to_string, 100
transpose, 55, 110

unique, 46
Unpacking, 36
unstack, 141
update, 56
upper, 64
utf-8, 78

value_counts, 46, 94, 168
values, 21
var, 49, 129, 133
variance, 129
vectorized, 109
verify_integrity, 114
virtualenv, 6

wide data, 136

Also Available

Beginning Python Programming

Treading on Python: Beginning Python Programming[26] by Matt Harrison is the complete book to teach you Python fast. Designed to up your Python game by covering the basics:

- Interpreter Usage
- Types
- Sequences
- Dictionaries
- Functions
- Indexing and Slicing
- File Input and Output
- Classes
- Exceptions
- Importing
- Libraries
- Testing
- And more ...

Reviews

> Matt Harrison gets it, admits there are undeniable flaws and schisms in Python, and guides you through it in short and to the point examples. I bought both Kindle and paperback editions to always have at the ready for continuing to learn to code in Python.
>
> S. Oakland

> This book was a great intro to Python fundamentals, and was very easy to read. I especially liked all the tips and suggestions scattered throughout to help the reader program Pythonically :)
>
> W. Dennis

---

[26] http://hairysun.com/books/tread/

Also Available

You don't need 1600 pages to learn Python

Last time I was using Python when Lutz's book Learning Python had only 300 pages. For whatever reasons, I have to return to Python right now. I have discovered that the same book today has 1600 pages.

Fortunately, I discovered Harrison's books. I purchased all of them, both Kindle and paper. Just few days later I was on track.

Harrison's presentation is just right. Short and clear. There is no 50 pages about the Zen and philosophy of using if-then-else construct. Just facts.

A. Customer

Treading on Python: Vol 2: Intermediate Python

Treading on Python: Vol 2: Intermediate Python[27] by Matt Harrison is the complete book on intermediate Python. Designed to up your Python game by covering:

- Functional Programming
- Lambda Expressions
- List Comprehensions

ALSO AVAILABLE

- Generator Comprehensions
- Iterators
- Generators
- Closures
- Decorators
- And more ...

Reviews

> Complete! All you must know about Python Decorators: theory, practice, standard decorators.
>
> All written in a clear and direct way and very affordable price.
>
> Nice to read in Kindle.
>
> F. De Arruda (Brazil)

> This is a very well written piece that delivers. No fluff and right to the point, Matt describes how functions and methods are constructed, then describes the value that decorators offer.
>
> ...
>
> Highly recommended, even if you already know decorators, as this is a very good example of how to explain this syntax illusion to others in a way they can grasp.
>
> J Babbington

> Decorators explained the way they SHOULD be explained ...
>
> There is an old saying to the effect that "Every stick has two ends, one by which it may be picked up, and one by which it may not." I believe that most explanations of decorators fail because they pick up the stick by the wrong end.
>
> What I like about Matt Harrison's e-book "Guide to: Learning Python Decorators" is that it is structured in

---

[27] http://hairysun.com/books/treadvol2/

the way that I think an introduction to decorators should be structured. It picks up the stick by the proper end…

Which is just as it should be.

S. Ferg

This book will clear up your confusions about functions even before you start to read about decoration at all. In addition to getting straight about scope, you'll finally get clarity about the difference between arguments and parameters, positional parameters, named parameters, etc. The author concedes that this introductory material is something that some readers will find "pedantic," but reports that many people find it helpful. He's being too modest. The distinctions he draws are essential to moving your programming skills beyond doing a pretty good imitation to real fluency.

R. Careago

Printed in Great Britain
by Amazon